Birds&Blooms
Everyday Birdwatching Stories

*House wren
page 107*

Contents

INTRODUCTION V

SPRING
Returning Friends..................... 6
Room for Rent 70

SUMMER
In Full Bloom...........................76
8 Flowers
   Hummingbirds Love 136

FALL
Autumn Amazement 142
Host a Peanut Party...............192

WINTER
Let It Snow.............................198
Welcome Winter Birds 252

White-crowned sparrow,
page 46

A *Birds & Blooms* Book

© 2021 RDA Enthusiast Brands, LLC.
1610 N. 2nd St., Suite 102, Milwaukee, WI
53212-3906

ISBN:
978-1-62145-747-3
(Hardcover)
978-1-62145-748-0
(Paperback)
978-1-62145-595-0
(Epub)

Library of Congress Control Number:
2021938564

Component Number: 118500106H

We are committed to both the quality of
our products and the service we provide
to our customers. We value your comments,
so please feel free to contact us at
TMBBookTeam@TrustedMediaBrands.com.

For more *Birds & Blooms* products, visit us at
our website: www.birdsandblooms.com.

Text, photography and illustrations for
Everyday Birdwatching Stories are based on
articles previously published in *Birds & Blooms*
magazine (www.birdsandblooms.com).

Printed in the United States of America
10 9 8 7 6 5 4 3 2 1
(Hardcover)
10 9 8 7 6 5 4 3 2 1
(Paperback)

Image Credits

Getty: **front cover** Saddako

Shutterstock: **196** Angel72; **255 t** windu

iStockPhoto: **252** ferrantraite

Other: **back cover l** Glenn Traver; **back cover
r** Karol Habersetzer; **i** Scott Diedrich; **ii** Travis
Bonovsky; **iv** Rebecca Granger; **v** Andy Raupp;
70 Marie Read; **71** Kathleen Colligan; **72** Steve
and Dave Maslowski; **73** Dave Welling; **74**
Roland Jordahl; **136** William Friggle; **137**
Michael Castelli; **138 tc** Roslynn Long; **138 bl**
Maureen Szuniewicz; **139** Mid Stutsman; **140 t**
Barbara Houlihan; **140 b** Tarek Aoun; **141** Roy
Western; **192-193** Marie Schmidt; **194** Janet
Wachter; **195** Kathy Adams Clark/KAC
Productions; **197** Bonnie Myszka; **252** Jim
McCollum; **253** Jason Baden; **254** Steve and
Dave Maslowski; **255 c** Nancy MacDonald; **255
b** Perky Pet

Nashville warbler

Welcome!

Spotting a favorite bird or finding a completely new visitor in your yard are truly cherished moments. *Everyday Birdwatching Stories* features *Birds & Blooms* readers telling the tales of winged friends they've found—from finches to owls and everything in between—in every season. Plus, special sections at the end of each chapter help you attract birds to your yard. So relax, take a seat by a window, and savor these heartwarming bird tales and lovely photos.

—THE EDITORS OF
BIRDS & BLOOMS MAGAZINE

Returning Friends

Spring brings brilliant blooms, cheery songs, adorable fledglings and even a few exciting, unusual backyard visitors.

BRING IN BLUE JAYS
Draw blue jays into your backyard with peanuts or sunflower seeds in a tray feeder. All birds need water, too, so consider adding a birdbath to your yard.

My deck is my photography studio. One spring day, I set peanuts all around me and caught a photo of this blue jay.

Anthony Quinn SILVER SPRING, MARYLAND

Last year I saw quite a few beautiful western tanagers. I even captured photographs of some of them.

Sylvia Hooper
CANON CITY, COLORADO

I captured this picture of a black-headed grosbeak during a soft rain. I love photographing birds on cloudy days when there are fewer shadows to detract from the bird. A migrant species, this grosbeak is one of my favorites. Its arrival confirms winter is over, spring has begun and summer is on its way.

Mark Schmitt
WOFFORD HEIGHTS, CALIFORNIA

Apparently American robins can have a case of the Mondays, too! I caught this one foraging on the ground early in the morning, when it decided to take a break for a big yawn.

Jessica Nelson
DAYTON, MARYLAND

In Canada the winters are often very long. I always look forward to the arrival of spring, and one of the earliest visitors to show up is the mountain bluebird. I love their bright blue color. It reminds me of warm summer days with deep blue skies.

Wendall Shaw
CARDSTON, ALBERTA

When I moved here, I didn't realize how much it would become a paradise for me and the birds! I love feeding and taking pictures of my visitors, such as this male purple finch.

Michelle Summers PARADISE, TEXAS

My son and I took a recent trip to Buffalo, Wyoming, and found these young great horned owls in a secluded area outside of town. They seemed as curious about us as we were about them. After observing them from about 10 yards away, we went home for the night. The owls, on the other hand, stayed in place and most likely took care of the local garden snake population (much to the dismay of my 4-year-old snake hunter).

Trevor Ruff BARABOO, WISCONSIN

Easter weekend last year was dreary. A large system stalled over the state, and it was pouring rain all day Saturday. Sunday was better, but thick fog lay across Indianapolis most of the morning. Needless to say, it was difficult to get out to take photos. After Easter dinner I decided to squeeze in some photo time and hung the thistle feeder in the redbud tree. This American goldfinch was accommodating, and I was happy to get a few memorable shots.

Mike Timmons
INDIANAPOLIS, INDIANA

I lucked out and spotted this scarlet tanager sitting pretty in the sunlight while I was out for a walk. I'm always glad when I bring my camera along with me.

Phillip Werman
NEW YORK CITY,
NEW YORK

TWO HUES

Male scarlet tanagers look very different from females in summer. They are striking red with black wings, while the females are a muted olive yellow. In winter, the males fade to dull yellow and look like the females again.

I caught this white-throated sparrow taking a dip in my small birdbath, which I had just filled with water. There are so many types of sparrows, I often find it difficult to identify them. But the yellow lore spot between the eye and bill gave away the identity of this happy swimmer.

Kimberly Miskiewicz
RALEIGH, NORTH CAROLINA

I always look forward to the first hummingbird of the season—and last year was no exception. We put out our hummingbird feeders during the first weekend in April, which is a little early for us. Lo and behold, this broad-tailed hummingbird showed up early! I was delighted to see the other hummingbirds follow suit just a week later.

Kristen Clark
TIJERAS, NEW MEXICO

When I turned to start my walk at a park, I noticed a male eastern bluebird perched a few feet away. I quickly prepared my camera—and I couldn't believe the bluebird didn't move.

Ginny Phillips OLATHE, KANSAS

LOOKING FOR LOVE

Male blue-winged warblers sing to defend a territory and attract their mate. They croon from the tops of tall shrubs or at the edges of fields when calling to female warblers.

I hurried down the trail to locate this blue-winged warbler after I heard its unmistakable raspy buzzing nearby. It was hamming it up on top of one of the smallest trees in the woods.

Dan Miller LAFAYETTE, INDIANA

Cedar waxwings visited me for the first time two years ago in May. They love my old mulberry tree! I hoped they would come back the next year, and I was thrilled to see more than 50 of them. It'd be wonderful if their return became a pattern.

Anita Stevens
FAIRMONT, WEST VIRGINIA

I snapped a photo of this regal great egret mother and her chick when I went to the Venice Area Audubon Rookery in Venice, Florida.

Donald Gettys
NORTH PORT, FLORIDA

I spotted
this western
bluebird in flight
near Ellensburg,
Washington. I've been
photographing birds
for a while now, and
pictures like this are
why I enjoy it!

Thomas Tully
SEATTLE, WASHINGTON

Fort Collins,
Colorado, is
a city that includes
many natural areas,
some within the high
prairie and Front Range
foothills of the Rocky
Mountains. Walking the
well-maintained trails
where I took this photo
of a female red-winged
blackbird is a wonderful
treat year-round.

Bill Robertson
FORT COLLINS,
COLORADO

As I made my way down to a trail, I spotted this lovely red-bellied woodpecker barely peeking out of its hole. When I shifted to the side of the tree, it finally emerged to check if I was still there.

William Friggle DENVER, PENNSYLVANIA

**YOU ARE
WHAT
YOU EAT**
A male house finch
gets his red color
from the amount
of pigment in the
food he eats.

I was so excited when I captured this photo of a house finch. I had been trying to get a picture of a bird in one of my trees, but every time they saw me, they would fly off—until this lucky moment.

Tanya Baker MCEWEN, TENNESSEE

Late last April

I was visiting the nearby Rotary Botanical Gardens when I spied this robin hopping around, looking and listening for breakfast. It took 15 minutes of quiet watching to capture this moment!

Marsha Mood
JANESVILLE, WISCONSIN

While out with my camera

on a cool, bright morning in the Sonoran Desert, I spied this curve-billed thrasher ducking into a staghorn cholla cactus. I approached quietly and found the bird rummaging around in a nest it had built in the heart of the cactus. I set my camera on its tripod and waited for the thrasher to surface. I was ready when it popped its head out of the safety of its nest!

Amanda Miller
PEORIA, ARIZONA

I had been looking for hummingbirds along the San Joaquin River, when this western kingbird came and perched on a wild tree-tobacco plant. I like how the colors of the blossoms compliment the color of his breast.

Mike Allred
FRESNO, CALIFORNIA

When I first started bird-watching, I took my binoculars and camera far and wide, looking for new birds to photograph. I would learn to identify more bird species by looking them up in field guides. I was surprised one spring when I noticed some of the warblers I'd traveled to see were visiting my front yard! A yellow warbler stopped in for a few insects living on the tree.

Debbie Miller
DEKALB, ILLINOIS

Early one gorgeous spring morning, at the Felts Audubon
Preserve in Palmetto, Florida, my wife and I were observing a pileated woodpecker
nest. Three very hungry chicks were struggling to poke their heads out in an effort
to get Mom's attention. Finally, the trio managed to emerge, and the feeding
began. The chicks fledged a few days after this shot was taken.

Ed Boos ST. PETERSBURG, FLORIDA

A LONG JOURNEY

Canada warblers trek more than 3,000 miles from South America to spring breeding grounds in the U.S. and Canada. Look for them in shrubby, deciduous and mixed-conifer forests, and on woodland slopes.

A few springs ago, we had a late-season blizzard. In the weeks following the storm, eight new bird species I'd never seen showed up on our property. This male Canada warbler was one of them. He sat in the dogwood bush outside my window, just resting and looking around. I love how his colors pop against the background of new grass after the snowmelt.

Susan Boyce PICKETT, WISCONSIN

I took this picture of a Cape May warbler as it migrated through our area.

Gus Asimenios
CHEEKTOWAGA, NEW YORK

When I was photographing hummingbirds at Stumpy Lake Natural Area, I managed to get a few frames of this blue-gray gnatcatcher with a caterpillar. I didn't even know the caterpillar was there until I transferred the picture onto my home computer! I'm not sure whether it became a meal for the small bird, but it made for a good photo.

Mark Winterstein
VIRGINIA BEACH, VIRGINIA

This purple finch perched on the soft maple tree by our patio before flying down to enjoy a meal of black oil sunflower seeds and peanut butter spread on pine cones. I love how its color perfectly matches the maple buds that were just beginning to open.

Joe Stambaugh
ASTORIA, ILLINOIS

My wife has always wanted to see a burrowing owl, so last year we took a trip to Florida. Once there, we were fortunate enough to find two parks with multiple nesting pairs. Of the hundreds of photos I took, this one is my favorite! Next year, we plan to go to Florida a month later than last time, so we can see and photograph the fledglings.

Rick Hamilton
WESTMINSTER,
MARYLAND

Blue jays are the perfect birds to photograph thanks to their iridescent feathers, soft blue crown and majestic size. This beautiful jay was calling attention to itself while perched on our flowering crabapple tree. These birds have so many different and interesting songs!

Karol Habersetzer WEST BEND, WISCONSIN

FOUR LOOKS

The yellow-rumped warbler has four forms, all with distinct appearances. Myrtles (shown here) are found in the East and far North, while Audubons' can be seen in the West. The other two forms are found in Mexico and Guatemala.

I was enjoying a warm, lovely North Carolina spring day when I looked toward a walnut tree and saw an active adult male yellow-rumped warbler protecting the bird feeder I had hung.

Phylicia Clemens LEXINGTON, NORTH CAROLINA

It took many thousands of pictures to learn how to photograph birds well, but sometimes there are moments when things just fall into place. Baltimore orioles are regular visitors to our farm, but I couldn't get them to come within shot. I sat outside waiting for such an opportunity, and two birds appeared on the honeysuckle. Was I lucky, or what?

Robin Seeber
WEST ALEXANDER,
PENNSYLVANIA

I captured this photo of a brown thrasher in early spring in Ohio. These birds are so neat to watch and listen to in my backyard—each one has its own distinct appearance and sound.

Ashley Buckler
BETHEL, OHIO

This beautiful prothonotary warbler photo was taken during the annual birding festival at Indiana Dunes State Park. The bird had been eluding photographers all weekend, showing up only occasionally. But on the final day of the festival I was one of two lucky photographers to catch it singing outside a birdhouse near a small bog. The other photographer was from England—he had traveled all the way there just to spot the reclusive prothonotary.

David Meachum
MEMPHIS, INDIANA

I took this photo of a ruby-crowned kinglet at Bay Beach Wildlife Sanctuary in Green Bay, Wisconsin. It's an amazing place! Last spring, spotting a spruce tree that had a few kinglets in it, I backed into an adjacent bush and waited for one to pass my camera's line of sight. Kinglets are very jumpy birds, and they sit still for only a second.

Jeff Weymier
HOBART, WISCONSIN

Every single spring and throughout most of the year,

50 to 100 hummingbirds, like this male Calliope, visit my 11 feeders. They drink just about 2 gallons of sugar water per day! April is my favorite month because I've had as many as six species show up then—Anna's, rufous, Calliope, black-chinned, Allen's and a single Costa's.

Elijah Gildea REDDING, CALIFORNIA

I captured this photo of a male blue grosbeak at a campground near my home. It's a migratory bird in my area, and a very welcome one. Later I spotted a nest site a little farther away that I was careful not to disturb.

Mark Schmitt WOFFORD HEIGHTS, CALIFORNIA

The western tanager is one of the most colorful birds in Utah's Colorado Plateau. I named this colorful specimen Spot for the unusual orange markings on its body. It began drinking from one of my oriole feeders—something I'd never seen before. Later, two males in their first spring and three females who had been watching Spot sampled the nectar, too. I was amused by this apparently learned bird behavior.

Allen Livingston
HUNTINGTON, UTAH

The stately little Carolina chickadee never ceases to amaze me. I love its songs and the way it zips by to pick up a snack. Such a fun bird to have in the backyard.

Jean Owens
PARIS, TENNESSEE

MIXED FLOCKS

During migration and in winter, it's common for Carolina chickadees to associate with flocks of tufted titmice, white-breasted nuthatches and other birds.

Digital photography

has greatly increased my enjoyment of both birding and taking photos. If you don't recognize the bird you photographed, there's always an image to help identify it. That's how I determined this was a gray catbird.

Carl Muehlemeyer
BROOMFIELD, COLORADO

This little song sparrow landed on
a redbud tree branch, its breakfast in beak, early one morning. Song sparrows are such a conspicuous part of spring. Whenever I come upon one boldly standing on its perch, singing its song, it makes all the glorious colors of spring seem much brighter.

Stuart Allison
CORONADO, CALIFORNIA

When I began pursuing photography a few years ago,
I dreamed of getting a shot of a bird in my backyard crabapple tree while it
was in bloom. Last year, I waited and waited as the sun slowly set, and I captured
this lovely white-throated sparrow as it sat and snacked on the tree's blossoms.
Patience and hard work really paid off!

Janelle Pitula OSWEGO, ILLINOIS

MASTERFUL MIMIC
A northern mockingbird is constantly picking up new sounds—around 200 or so in the course of its life!

The range of sounds a northern mockingbird can make is amazing, and I'm fortunate to have one of these wonderful birds frequent my backyard. I think this photograph exemplifies what mockingbirds do better than any other bird: sing their hearts out. I especially love the way the sunlight illuminates the inside of its open beak.

Steven Biegler NORTH BELLMORE, NEW YORK

Every time I look at this photo, I smile. Serendipitously, I clicked my camera shutter in the split second that they "kissed." Capturing this magical moment between a male and female northern cardinal has been on my photography bucket list for a while. I'm so glad I finally reached my goal.

Kerry Loving
CARLISLE, IOWA

The Florida scrub-jay lives only in Florida. For the past five years, my wife and I have visited a site where a family of three to five of these naturally curious birds resides. During one visit, I walked away from my camera and was surprised when three scrub-jays landed on it. Fortunately, I had a hand-held camera with me and I was able to capture the moment.

Edward Boos
SCALY MOUNTAIN,
NORTH CAROLINA

An American robin stopped by our endless water fountain one bright and sunny afternoon for a quick dip. It went around the top of the fountain several times, as if trying to find the perfect spot.

Kimberly Miskiewicz
RALEIGH, NORTH CAROLINA

I caught a picture of this Kirtland's warbler at Grant Park in Chicago, Illinois. I was surprised to see this bird, since it's a rare sight around here.

Jamie Burning
NILES, ILLINOIS

ALONG THE WAY

Kirtland's warblers nest in the upper Midwest, but sometimes they can be spotted as they migrate north from their warm winter homes in the Bahamas.

Every spring, elegant trogons come up to southeast Arizona to nest in wooded canyons. I photographed this one in Huachuca Canyon near Sierra Vista.

Dale James PRESCOTT, ARIZONA

I always look forward to the return of the yellow-headed blackbirds in the spring. Most of the time they hang out in the trees, but every so often I catch them down in the grass, as with this male.

Missi Gregorius POST FALLS, IDAHO

I've been amazed by the graceful beauty of black-necked stilts for a few years, but I never managed a decent shot until recently. A local birder pointed me in the right direction and, after several outings, I captured this image with the sunset glowing in the background.

Clay Guthrie
EAST PRAIRIE, MISSOURI

This gray catbird visited our yard last spring, and it always chose to perch at the top of the white spruce tree. I took this photo on a cool morning, so when it fluffed its feathers, it became even more attractive than usual.

B.J. Lanich
WAUSAUKEE, WISCONSIN

I like to drive around the San Diego area looking for birds. I was hoping to spot bald eagles when this young red-tailed hawk landed in a tree right next to where I was parked. I slowly got out of the car, and it let me photograph it before it took flight.

Tom Applegate
SANTEE, CALIFORNIA

I spotted this female orchard oriole hanging out on the bleeding hearts in my backyard. A new bird seems to arrive every day during the first few weeks of spring!

Michael Berg
COAL VALLEY, ILLINOIS

KNOCK, KNOCK!
Woodpeckers have a special bone in their skulls that wraps around their brain. It works like a seat belt, protecting their tiny brains from damage.

While birding a local path, I heard a woodpecker land on a tree and begin to drum. I walked stealthily toward the sound and, rounding a bend, I saw a pileated woodpecker hitching around the tree. I watched it for a few moments before it flew off. Pileateds are super shy and wary of humans, so to come within a few feet of this bird was an unforgettable encounter.

Alicia Brown OZARK, ALABAMA

I love getting outside and seeing all the beauty nature has to offer, such as this white-crowned sparrow on my weeping cherry tree.

Rebecca Granger BANCROFT, MICHIGAN

A pair of tree swallows were building a nest in our nest box and decided to take a break on my wind spinner. They went around and around, as if they were enjoying their own merry-go-round!

Lisa Faith
ANTIOCH, ILLINOIS

Anyone who knew my Grandma Bernice knew she loved birds and that her favorite was the mountain bluebird. When I was a kid, we would go check her nest boxes to make sure they were clean and ready for new bluebird families. Now, years later, I think of my grandma every time I see a mountain bluebird, especially during spring.

Brenda Kerttu
NAPLES, IDAHO

With the vivid colors of this male yellow warbler against the pink crabapple blooms, you wouldn't guess I took this shot on a rainy, drab day. I was actually trying to photograph a male Baltimore oriole when this handsome fellow popped into the picture. I was glad to get a shot of this beautiful bird.

Lynn Cleveland
FRANKFORT, NEW YORK

Last migration season, I was blessed to see white-crowned sparrows making their way north, and I noticed many more that spring than in years past!

Rebecca Granger
BANCROFT, MICHIGAN

FLASHY COLORS

They're known for the bright plumage on their dome, but red-headed woodpeckers are equally striking below the neck. Their white bodies with large, black accents have earned them the nickname flying checkerboards.

Red-headed woodpeckers were my dad's favorite birds, so they will always have a special place in my heart. They fly though northwestern Indiana but don't stay long. I quietly sneaked around to get a clear view of this one, but it flew off after only two photos. I was disappointed until I saw how this shot turned out.

Paul Lawson NEW CARLISLE, INDIANA

I captured this American redstart during a stroll in Hammonasset Beach State Park in Madison, Connecticut. To get the best light possible, I take walks in early morning and try to position myself in a spot where the quality, character and direction of light are in my favor. Then I wait quietly for birds to enter the good light. I use bird photography as a form of meditation, so being patient is actually the easy part.

William Canosa BRANFORD, CONNECTICUT

Before heading home after a day of bird-watching on the trails at South Llano River State Park, I stopped at a bird blind near the park's entrance. The temperature was in the 90s, so this water feature was very busy! A male painted bunting and a female orchard oriole sharing the dripping water provided a very colorful picture of the action.

Ron Newhouse
BRYAN, TEXAS

While I searched for spring migrants, this white-breasted nuthatch landed on a branch just a few feet away from me.

Walker Catlett
CHARLOTTESVILLE,
VIRGINIA

I never have as much time to look for birds as I'd like, but luckily this yellow warbler found me one day. I grabbed my camera and stepped out onto the porch, patiently waiting for the bird to move into the light so I could get my perfect photo.

Janelle Pitula
OSWEGO, ILLINOIS

Not long after I mounted a sturdy cedar birdhouse on a railing, a pair of house wrens showed up to raise a family. It was amazing to watch how much care the wrens put into feeding their hungry babies. Every morning they brought grubs and caterpillars.

Chris Hiller
SLINGER, WISCONSIN

GREAT MIGRATION

Cattle egrets are native to Africa but somehow made their way to South America. First spotted in the United States in 1941, they now live all across the country.

I photographed this adult cattle egret in its mating plumage. These birds enjoy fields where cows are present, and they're often found eating the insects that the large beasts stir up in the fields.

David Haas CANTON, MICHIGAN

This eastern meadowlark was serenading a field when I took its photo. They have such a pretty song. Sometimes it's nice to roll down the car window, drive slowly down a country road and listen to them.

Peter Brannon TAMPA, FLORIDA

When eastern bluebirds return to nest in our yard, we eagerly await the fledging process as adults work tirelessly to feed the hungry mouths at the opening of the bluebird house. We missed the youngsters leaving the house, but I managed to capture this moment when one of the parents was feeding a fledgling.

Dolan Trout
MONTGOMERY, ALABAMA

My favorite backyard bird by far is this downy woodpecker that I've named Spunk. It is all personality!

Nicole Eckstein
MACHESNEY PARK, ILLINOIS

As I strolled through the Hank's Meadow loop trail in the Quabbin Reservoir, I spotted a female eastern towhee (shown here). Just a few minutes later the male showed up!

Stephen Shelasky
LONGMEADOW, MASSACHUSETTS

Roseate spoonbills are my favorite birds. Several were in the water when I spotted this one flying in to join them at Little Estero Island Critical Wildlife Area in Fort Myers Beach, Florida.

Tom Miller
TOWSON, MARYLAND

BOLD BILLS
A roseate spoonbill sifts up tiny fish, shrimp and snails by sweeping its wide, slightly open bill back and forth through the shallow water.

Cactus wrens at the Arizona-Sonora Desert Museum in Tucson were busy with their babies in a saguaro. I think this photo is so funny! I tried to come up with a caption and settled for "The kids have left home."

Diane Barone BOISE, IDAHO

Last year I came upon this male lazuli bunting singing his heart out. When he stopped for a bit of grass seed, I captured a snapshot showing some closeup details. I was really surprised to see the blue extending down his legs.

Douglas Beall SALEM, OREGON

My mother, my aunt and I have attended the Tawas Point Birding Festival for the past 15 years. Mom was unable to make it to the festival last spring, but I took pictures of everything of interest, and I shared them with her. This picture of an American redstart was definitely one of her favorites.

Bonnie Walraven
BAY CITY, MICHIGAN

This newly hatched killdeer had not learned to walk well yet, but when I came near, it took off, running after its mother. They looked alike, except that the young one's feathers were quite ruffled. The hatchling also ran on its tippy-toes!

Jean Watson
NEWBERN, ALABAMA

Thrilled is an understatement of how I felt when I spotted this male northern parula while walking the McDade trail in northeast Pennsylvania. He was very hard to find and photograph— I could hear him better than I could see him. But for a few seconds he let me take a couple of shots!

Nancy Tully
EAST STROUDSBURG, PENNSYLVANIA

BUZZY TUNES

Northern parulas are often vocal during migration, singing a distinct buzzy trill.

South Florida is like a bird highway during migration. I took this picture last March when the black-and-white warblers arrived from their wintering grounds.

Frank Garcia
HOLLYWOOD, FLORIDA

On my farm in southern Ontario, an old tree sits right outside my front door. It was a beautiful spring day when the Baltimore orioles stopped to check out the apple blossoms. And as you can see, they are quite acrobatic! I had to pick up my camera and take a few photos of the flashes of orange going from branch to branch.

Karen Root CAMPBELLVILLE, ONTARIO

Every spring we travel to Monterey, Virginia, to photograph birds.
This male scarlet tanager was hanging around an old apple tree eating insects. I
took what might be my best shot ever. I have seen lots of scarlet tanager photos,
but none with the same color contrast and framed within such beautiful blossoms.

Troy Baker CONCORD, NORTH CAROLINA

A yellow-throated warbler was singing in an oak in our front yard. I sat near a ginkgo tree listening to its song. In time, the warbler landed right in front of me on the ginkgo, and I snapped this photo. The soft light added a nice, peaceful tone.

Brian Lowry
SCOTTSBURG, INDIANA

Since falling in love with birding and amateur photography, I realized every shot taken is truly a once-in-a-lifetime event. After watching two tufted titmice flirt all afternoon, the male handed his precious mate a morsel of food. She accepted it and she seemed shyly appreciative of his actions. How sweet!

Anita Durst
JACKSONVILLE, FLORIDA

CHOOSING A HOME

Tufted titmice nest in tree cavities, but instead of carving out their own holes, they use abandoned woodpecker nests.

Last spring, a pair of blue jays hatched five young on our back porch. About the time the juveniles were so big they barely fit in the nest, the parents began making a terrible racket. Outside, I discovered three of the five young ones hopping around the yard, and a fourth ready to leave the nest. No. 5 lingered before joining the rest. I caught this one just as it got off the ground.

Karen Green
MOUNT PLEASANT, MICHIGAN

HAWK MIMICS
Blue jays can imitate hawk calls and may do so to trick other birds into thinking a hawk is around.

Our first winter in Minnesota was one of our longest ever, and we were ecstatic to see spring arrive. It was thrilling to see birds stop for a rest on their northern migrations, especially the eastern myrtle variety of yellow-rumped warblers. We loved seeing them make visits to our feeders for nearly a month before they moved on.

Martin Gilchrist
MILACA, MINNESOTA

During inclement weather on a late April day,

14 Audubon's yellow-rumped warblers paused from their northward migration to stop at the suet feeders in my small yard. I enjoyed four days of photographing them before the weather broke and they continued north.

Gregory Vinyard TALENT, OREGON

Photographing a rose-breasted grosbeak was very special because I don't see many of these. The light was perfect as it sat in the dogwood tree in my front yard. I saw it for a couple of days, and then the gorgeous grosbeak continued its journey.

Alan Tucker BUCKHANNON, WEST VIRGINIA

This family of western kingbirds shared a meal in late spring when the dragonflies were active. In unison, the juveniles appealed to the parent for a fresh nibble. The color of their open beaks is really stunning.

Douglas Beall
CAMP SHERMAN, OREGON

It was a beautiful late spring day when I spotted this Swainson's thrush picking berries in the Skagit Valley in Washington. I love the brightness of the fruits against the muted colors of the thrush.

Adrienne Smith
CONCRETE, WASHINGTON

Indigo buntings are one of my favorite local birds, and I have struggled to get a good shot of them because they seem to be constantly moving. I went to my favorite spot to watch them and picked a perch to focus on. Sure enough, this beauty came and sat just long enough for me to snap a photo.

Clay Guthrie
EAST PRAIRIE, MISSOURI

THISTLE LOVER

Attract indigo buntings by offering thistle seed and brushy patches in which they can forage for seeds.

I live on a huge migration path for warblers and other birds. Seeing red-eyed vireos is always a highlight for me. After two weeks of searching, I found what I'd been looking for. This vireo flew off as quickly as it came, but I was happy I got a few shots of it in the moment.

Daniel Draudt
BUFFALO, NEW YORK

One spring morning, my friend Gary and I visited Rocky Mountain Arsenal National Wildlife Refuge. A herd of bison roams there, so you're required to stay in your car. As we drove, I spotted the bright colors of a Bullock's oriole in a clump of cottonwood trees. While snapping photos out the open car window, I captured this shot.

Carl Muehlemeyer BROOMFIELD, COLORADO

The sandy soil of Cape Coral, Florida, makes it a favorite nesting spot for burrowing owls. Two years ago, I found an active burrow near my winter home and photographed a female guarding her nest. When I returned last year, both a male and female were home. I waited patiently until the lovebirds hopped to their perch, and I captured this shot—a photograph two long years in the making!

Barbara Morris UTICA, NEW YORK

My husband spoke to me in a soft, hurried voice: "Honey, don't move." I froze. I looked at him and saw him point up. I carefully raised my eyes and saw a yellow-throated warbler. It was hard to contain my excitement! My husband urged me to add it to our farm list—it was number 61. The warbler came back for several days, and we watched it munch on sunflower chips at our feeder and gather horse hair. We hope to see this species around here again.

Robin Seeber
WEST ALEXANDER,
PENNSYLVANIA

Designing and building my garden to attract wildlife in Orlando, Florida, is a work in progress. Cardinals often make an early morning appearance. This beautiful female perched in my spicy jatropha tree before she went to one of the feeders. Her songs bring life to my yard.

Gilberto Sanchez
ORLANDO, FLORIDA

A RARE SINGER

It's uncommon for female songbirds to sing, but the female northern cardinal is one of the few that does, usually doing so on her nest.

Room for Rent

Discover which cavity dwellers you can attract to your backyard.

by Kenn and Kimberly Kaufman

Red-breasted sapsuckers, as well as many other sapsuckers and woodpeckers, excavate wood cavities, which many kinds of birds reuse.

For parent birds, raising a nest full of babies can be a risky project. With predators lurking around every corner, many parents hide their nests among dense foliage or in tall grass for protection. Another approach is to put it inside a tree. This cavity-nesting strategy is practiced by all kinds of birds, including some that you can attract to your backyard.

The Builders

Left alone, a mature tree may develop natural cavities in spots where branches have fallen off or large limbs have decayed from within. But some birds don't wait around for these cavities to develop—they make their own. Members of the woodpecker family are expert homebuilders. They usually excavate their own nest holes, choosing spots in dead trees or limbs. They're quite industrious about it, too. Typically, a pair of woodpeckers will dig a new nest hole for each new brood that they raise. In fall, they also dig holes to roost in during winter. Because they tend to keep excavating new holes instead of reusing old ones, they leave behind ready-made nest sites for many other birds.

Fix-Up Artists

Most birds don't have the chisel-shaped bills of woodpeckers, so they aren't quite as thoroughly well-equipped for excavating in

Attracting cheery house wrens to your backyard is easy with a manmade birdhouse.

Prothonotary warblers are one of the few warblers that will use a nest box.

dead wood. But some cavity nesters are willing to enlarge or modify existing small holes, and sometimes create their own. Chickadees, with their tiny bills, don't look as if they could create their own nest cavities, but they often do, enlarging a small knothole or digging a complete hole in soft, decaying wood. Nuthatches may modify existing holes or dig new ones. The oak titmouse on the West Coast will alter holes to suit its needs, but its eastern cousin, the tufted titmouse, seems to simply use holes as it finds them.

Popular Tenants

A standard birdhouse, or nest box, is simply an artificial version of a natural tree cavity. Several popular birds have adapted to nest boxes, giving backyard birders abundant opportunities for up-close views. Bluebirds are found all across the continent, and all three species—eastern, western and mountain—raise their young either in natural cavities or in nest boxes. The bluebird's popularity has been a bonanza for the tree swallow, another cavity nester, which uses holes of the same size.

The purple martin is another classic birdhouse species found in

5 TIPS FOR APPEALING TO CAVITY DWELLERS

1. Leave dead wood standing where you can. Of course, some dead trees and dead limbs have to come down for safety's sake. But if they won't fall on people or property, standing pieces of dead wood can be magnets for woodpeckers, which dig nest cavities and then leave them for other birds to use.

2. Consider "planting" a dead tree. Kimberly once hauled in a couple of huge cottonwood logs,

dug 6-foot holes and "planted" the logs upright at the back of her yard. Within a couple of years, she had woodpeckers, chickadees, wrens and other birds nesting.

3. Go easy on the pesticides. Most cavity-nesting birds are insect-eaters. If you use poisons to kill insects in your yard, the birds may not have enough to eat.

4. Put up nest boxes. Don't have dead trees around? You can still attract many cavity nesters by

putting up boxes for them. It's best to plan for specific types of birds rather than putting up generic birdhouses that might not be appropriate.

5. Don't encourage competitors for nest sites. Nonnative birds such as house sparrows and European starlings often take over nest cavities from our native birds. If sparrows and starlings mob your bird feeders, it might be wise to stop feeding during nesting season.

Don't forget to
look for owls
nesting in tree
cavities, such as
this pygmy owl.

If you live near water, be sure to put out a house for wood ducks.

eastern North America. Practically all martins east of the Rockies now nest in multiroomed martin houses, sometimes with dozens of pairs in the same structure.

In the West, some martins still nest in the traditional way, in cavities in dead trees—or, in the absence of dead trees, in holes in giant cactuses.

The High-Wren District

Wrens are mostly shades of brown and gray, but they make up for their lack of bright colors with high-energy personalities and musical songs. Five species are cavity nesters. The house wren is widespread from coast to coast, while the Bewick's wren lives mainly in the West, and the

Carolina wren is most common in the Southeast. The tiny winter wren nests in the North Woods, while its close relative, the Pacific wren, resides in the Far West.

These birds loosely define a "cavity" for nesting. They will nest in standard tree holes or nest boxes, but they also use crevices in buildings, hollows among the

BIRDHOUSE GUIDELINES

SPECIES	DIMENSIONS*	HOLE	PLACEMENT	COLOR	NOTES
Eastern bluebird	5x5x8 in.	1½ in. centered 6 in. above floor	5-10 ft. high in the open; sunny area	light earth tones	likes open areas, especially facing a field
Tree swallow	5x5x6 in.	1 in. centered 4 in. above floor	5-8 ft. high in the open; sunny area 50-100% sun	light earth tones or gray	within 2 miles of pond or lake
Purple martin	Multiple apts. 6x6x6 ea. (minimum)	2⅛ in. hole 2¼ in. above floor	15-20 ft. high in the open	white	open yard without tall trees; near water
Tufted titmouse	4x4x8 in.	1 1/4 in.	4-10 ft. high	light earth tones	prefers to live in or near woods
Chickadee	4x4x8 in. or 5x5-in. base	1⅛ in. centered 6 in. above floor	4-8 ft. high	light earth tones	small tree thicket
Nuthatch	4x4x10 in.	1¼ in. centered 7½ in. above floor	12-25 ft. high on tree trunk	bark-covered or natural	prefers to live in or near woods
House wren	4x4x8 in. or 4x6-in. base	1 in. centered 6 in. above floor	5-10 ft. high on post or hung in tree	light earth tones or white	prefers lower branches of backyard trees
Northern flicker	7x7x18 in.	2½ in. centered 14 in. above floor	8-20 ft. high	light earth tones	put 4″ sawdust inside for nesting
Downy woodpecker	4x4x10 in.	1¼ in. centered 7½ in. above floor	12-25 ft. high on tree trunk	simulate a natural cavity	prefers own excavation; provide sawdust
Red-headed woodpecker	6x6x15 in.	2 in. centered 6-8 in. above floor	8-20 ft. high on post or tree trunk	simulate a natural cavity	needs sawdust for nesting
Wood duck	10x10x24 in.	4x3-in. elliptical 20 in. above floor	2-5 ft. high on post over water, or 12-40 ft. high on tree by water	light earth tones or natural	needs 3-4 in. of sawdust or shavings for nesting
American kestrel	10x10x24 in.	4x3-in. elliptical 20 in. above floor	12-40 ft. high on post or tree trunk	light earth tones or natural	needs open approach on edge of woodlot or in isolated tree
Screech-owl	10x10x24 in.	4x3-in. elliptical 20 in. above floor	12-40 ft. high on tree	light earth tones or natural	prefers open woods or edge of woodlot

* The birdhouse dimensions are width by length by height.

Note: With the exception of wrens and purple martins, birds do not tolerate swaying birdhouses. Birdhouses should be firmly anchored to a post, a tree or the side of a building.

Source: Garden Birds of America by George H. Harrison. Willow Creek Press, 1996.

roots of fallen trees, old flowerpots in sheds—just about any enclosed space. House wrens have even been found building nests in the pockets of trousers hanging on clotheslines!

Surprising Cavity Nesters

Several other types of birds are also among the cavity crew. Various kinds of owls nest in cavities, including little screech-owls, which may lurk in holes even in suburban backyards. The American kestrel uses tree holes or nest boxes in open country. Wood ducks adopt tree hollows or nest boxes close to the water; hooded mergansers and common goldeneyes are other cavity-nesting waterfowl.

Those are all fairly large birds, but our last two examples are tiny.

Of the 55 species of warblers in North America, only two nest in cavities: Lucy's warbler, a pale gray bird of southwestern deserts, and the prothonotary warbler, a golden sprite of southeastern swamps. They remind us that nature is full of surprises. They also remind us that, regardless of what your dentist might say, cavities can be good things!

In Full Bloom

As the sun glows and gardens blossom in stunning color, readers share stories of fascinating bird encounters.

This white ibis posed for its picture in a swampy area close to our Orlando, Florida, hotel. It and a number of other marsh dwellers were hunting for and feeding on some of the largest snails I've ever seen.

Noel Fillman MCDONALD, TENNESSEE

Several years ago, I was forced to rest at home after an injury. To keep busy, I started taking bird photos. I was stunned by what I found! I've counted over 60 bird species that have visited my yard. While I was waiting for a repairman, I sneaked out to my shed/photography studio to take advantage of the morning light. I was amazed to find this pair of Baltimore orioles in my blossoming cherry tree, waiting their turn for the feeder (and grape jelly). I quickly snapped several photos, and was so pleased to have gotten this very special shot.

Michael Berg
COAL VALLEY, ILLINOIS

While I was trying to capture an action shot of this hummingbird, it sat on the stem of a flower. I quietly said, "Please sit still." To my surprise, it looked right at me and lit up, doing exactly as I asked it to. After a few clicks, the hummingbird was gone.

Joyce Rickert
SALEM, OREGON

I frequently cut a melon in half and put it out on a feeder just to see who will turn up to eat. On this particular day, it was a gray catbird.

Keith Anderson
PONCA CITY, OKLAHOMA

FRUIT FAVES
Attract boisterous gray catbirds with a variety of popular fruit options—oranges and grape jelly are among their favorites.

One summer I went on vacation to the Georgia coast, where I got a glimpse of a painted bunting. For the rest of my vacation, I spent hours trying to photograph him. This was the best shot I got.

April Heatherton
CRAB ORCHARD, KENTUCKY

My neighbor grows sunflowers and opens up his fields to the community, and people come from all over the world to photograph them. I love it when a songbird like this indigo bunting poses for a portrait.

Donna Bourdon OOLTEWAH, TENNESSEE

On a rainy summer morning, I had given up hope of doing any real bird photography for the day because of poor lighting conditions. Hummingbirds had been visiting my garden, so I was disappointed that I probably wouldn't get a decent photo. Through the morning gloom, a beautiful yellow warbler landed right on the stem of one of my dahlias, like a summer gift.

Glenn Traver HANOVER TOWNSHIP, PENNSYLVANIA

Bald eagles frequently visit my backyard.

I can always tell when one is nearby because my feeders suddenly become completely vacant. It's interesting to see how in sync birds are with their surroundings. This particular eagle seemed to look at me and say, *Are you done yet?*

Cynthia Bowers
INNSBROOK, MISSOURI

These two blue jays were starting

an aerial courtship chase when I captured this photo. I've been studying jays for a few years. There is so very much about them to observe, especially when it comes to their group dynamics.

Isabelle Marozzo
NORLAND, ONTARIO

This photo was taken while we were on a hike in Bella Vista, Arkansas. Our family observed this great blue heron catching fish in the creek.

Dena Peckham
REEDS, MISSOURI

I was lucky to spot this cedar waxwing gulping down as many of these tiny crabapples as it could get. I love the brilliant color accents of these birds and how they chat to each other while tossing back berries by the dozens. They're amazing to watch.

Kat Durant
SMITHS FALLS, ONTARIO

A LITTLE PITCHY

The Kaufman field guide says yellow-headed blackbirds attract attention with flashy colors and terrible attempts at singing. The guide describes the song as "a few gurgles followed by a long, strangled buzzing noise."

When I lived in the Midwest, I saw yellow-headed blackbirds only on rare occasions. After moving to Colorado, I was thrilled to find several nesting pairs at the lake just down the road from my house. Now I watch them every spring and summer.

Wolfe Repass BROOMFIELD, COLORADO

NOISEMAKER
Woodpeckers tap and knock on dense tree trunks and other hard surfaces to try to attract a mate. A woodpecker can drum more than 8,000 times in just one day!

Meet Woody, a quirky red-headed woodpecker who ruled my backyard. I got such a kick out of photographing this bird! Its favorite spot was this driftwood that I kept filled with nuts.

Darla Young SHERIDAN, ARKANSAS

Seeing six juvenile eastern bluebirds in our birdbath was a dream come true! We first spotted bluebirds in our yard in the year 2015. My husband built a birdhouse for them at my urgent request, and they nested here in 2016. Ever since, bluebirds regularly visit the bath, but we've never seen so many at once!

Brenda Crouse
SOMERVILLE,
NEW BRUNSWICK

Being an avid nature photographer, I am always on the lookout for special moments like this, when these two American goldfinches went after the seeds in my sunflowers. One of them flew to the flower and then the other one came to check it out. What looks like a peaceful, loving moment was quite the opposite. They were actually fighting for position on the flower, and the brightly colored bird on the right was the eventual winner.

Ray Mueller
BEAVERCREEK, OHIO

One July day,

the air above the pond at Wisconsin's Horicon Marsh was filled with tree swallows and black terns. A juvenile black tern landed on a post and waited for about 10 minutes for a meal. As the parent arrived, the young bird called out and got a bug delivered right from the air.

Tom Wright
WALES, WISCONSIN

As I walked back to my

car after trying to photograph bald eagles, I saw some movement out of the corner of my eye. I found this house wren feeding her young and hunting for food nonstop. The food she brought to the nest was much larger than the little ones could handle. I wondered how they could eat so much!

Doug Day
AMELIA, OHIO

I took this photo of a young northern flicker in my backyard. It discovered my birdbath and could not get enough of it. I captured a series of photos from various angles around the bath, but nothing beats this funny one of the flicker when it really dove in.

Walter T. Day Jr. AUBURN HILLS, MICHIGAN

American bitterns are often difficult to spot, but when these young ones galumphed around the marsh, it gave me a prime opportunity to capture them in their typical pose of "I am just a reed." Bitterns will shift back and forth in sync with the marsh grasses swaying in the breeze. It's a fascinating survival skill that makes them tricky to spot.

Douglas Beall CAMP SHERMAN, OREGON

For several summers I've hoped to catch one of the bright American goldfinches that perch on our hollyhocks. My patience was rewarded with not one but three goldfinches: Daddy feeding his two young.

Bertha Bridge
CONCRETE, WASHINGTON

CHANGING COLORS
Goldfinches will start to molt in late summer, so be on the lookout as their bright gold begins to fade.

Three pairs of vermilion flycatchers worked the edges of a park near my home, swooping in to catch gnats and other tasty bugs. Each pair seemed to have its own section—a circuit of favorite perches on low tree branches. This bird returned time and time again to perch not 10 feet from where I stood with my camera. Vermilions are great fun to watch! Its amazing acrobatics show off its brilliant red head and breast feathers with every twist and turn.

James Capo
ORO VALLEY, ARIZONA

I captured this photo of a female Anna's hummingbird at a Rockin' Deep Purple salvia. I live in the Skagit Valley and am usually able to photograph Anna's in my backyard all throughout the year.

Jamie Bartram
SEDRO-WOOLLEY, WASHINGTON

A female broad-tailed hummingbird has nested in the same place in our front yard for three years now. Our office window has afforded me a unique opportunity to watch and observe this female as she raises her young.

Carol Galloway
CENTENNIAL, COLORADO

This Steller's jay had been eluding me for a long time. It was never still and always sat in the shadows. But on this day, it posed in the light for me. You can really see what colorful birds they are.

Kathy Port GARDNERVILLE, NEVADA

FLOWER FANS
Many birds flock to sunflowers, including cardinals, goldfinches, pine siskins, chickadees and house finches.

Every year I plant a few sunflowers for their beauty and as a treat for the birds. One late summer afternoon, this American goldfinch traveled from flower to flower, checking out the seeds. He perched on the tallest flower and looked around, almost as if he were surveying his kingdom.

Pamela Howard PORT DEPOSIT, MARYLAND

As I was getting ready to go to work, a friend called me and told me that he knew where a white ruby-throated hummingbird had been spotted in a neighboring county. It turned out to be almost completely leucistic, which made it even more special!

Kenny Nations
HEBER SPRINGS, ARKANSAS

Two of this northern mockingbird's babies stayed on the ground to be fed, but one always hopped up on the birdbath and fluttered for attention. The parent made sure they all got fed, going back and forth to the ground, then up to the birdbath. It was crazy to see how much they managed to stuff into those little cute mouths!

Barbara Rushing
HENRICO, VIRGINIA

My mother

loved hummingbirds, so I started photographing them for her. After watching them, I have come to enjoy their antics, too! I noticed this sweet female ruby-throated hummingbird darting among my flowers, so I grabbed my camera and followed her around the yard. She was nose deep in the daylily, and I waited for her to come out. To my surprise she turned around and took a seat in the daylily! I was lucky enough to get a few shots of her before she took off again.

Vickie Tuskan
EVELETH, MINNESOTA

This common yellowthroat

looked anything but common while it sang in a field of purple lupine in Rangeley, Maine. I especially like the glowing contrast of the bright yellow warbler with the rich violet of the flowers.

Christopher Ciccone
WOBURN,
MASSACHUSETTS

This male California quail hopped onto a boulder in our backyard to get a better view. He was surrounded by wild California poppies (our state flower). I grabbed my Canon EOS 7D camera with a 100-400mm lens and captured the moment. I enjoy nature photography and keep my camera ready for the unexpected, even in my backyard.

Philip Robertson LINCOLN, CALIFORNIA

I absolutely love pelicans. This one was trying to convince me that he was bashful, but I didn't believe him—I had just witnessed him fighting to get fish scraps that some fishermen were throwing away. His vibrant colors stood out against the water.

Cary Mathis FULTON, TEXAS

I glimpsed a cute family of barn swallows perched high in a tree near water. I thought wistfully, *It would be great if they were perched right there on that log.* When I returned the next day, that's where they were!

Dan Miller
LAFAYETTE, INDIANA

One of my favorite of all the North American wood warblers is the ovenbird. Its distinct song and unique appearance, as well as its characteristic confident walk, are all very captivating. This particular ovenbird happened to stop by my water feature just long enough to take a bath.

Greg Knadle
FALLS CHURCH, VIRGINIA

BELT IT OUT
Male ovenbirds love to sing—and they'll do it during the hottest part of the day, setting themselves apart from plenty of other songbirds.

I was lucky to capture this shot of two black-bellied whistling ducks squaring off against each other. A duck from each flock would fly up and challenge a duck from the other group. It was fascinating to watch.

Robert Broome
WINTER GARDEN,
FLORIDA

One September Saturday, I just happened to glimpse something large in a nearby tree. I ran and grabbed my camera and saw that it was a magnificent barred owl. It seemed to be asleep, and I quietly went outside to get a closer look. Just then, a neighborhood child made a loud noise and the owl woke up and looked around. Then it looked right at me and gave me this wink. What a great backyard visitor!

Cynthia Stackhouse
COLUMBUS, OHIO

One day, my wife and I were out on a hike and we noticed an acorn woodpecker collecting nuts and depositing them into an old tree branch. I took multiple snapshots, but some were out of focus, because I forgot to bring my tripod along. This one turned out the best, though, and caught the woodpecker with an acorn in his mouth. All the different colors really make the photograph.

David Scholl SALT LAKE CITY, UTAH

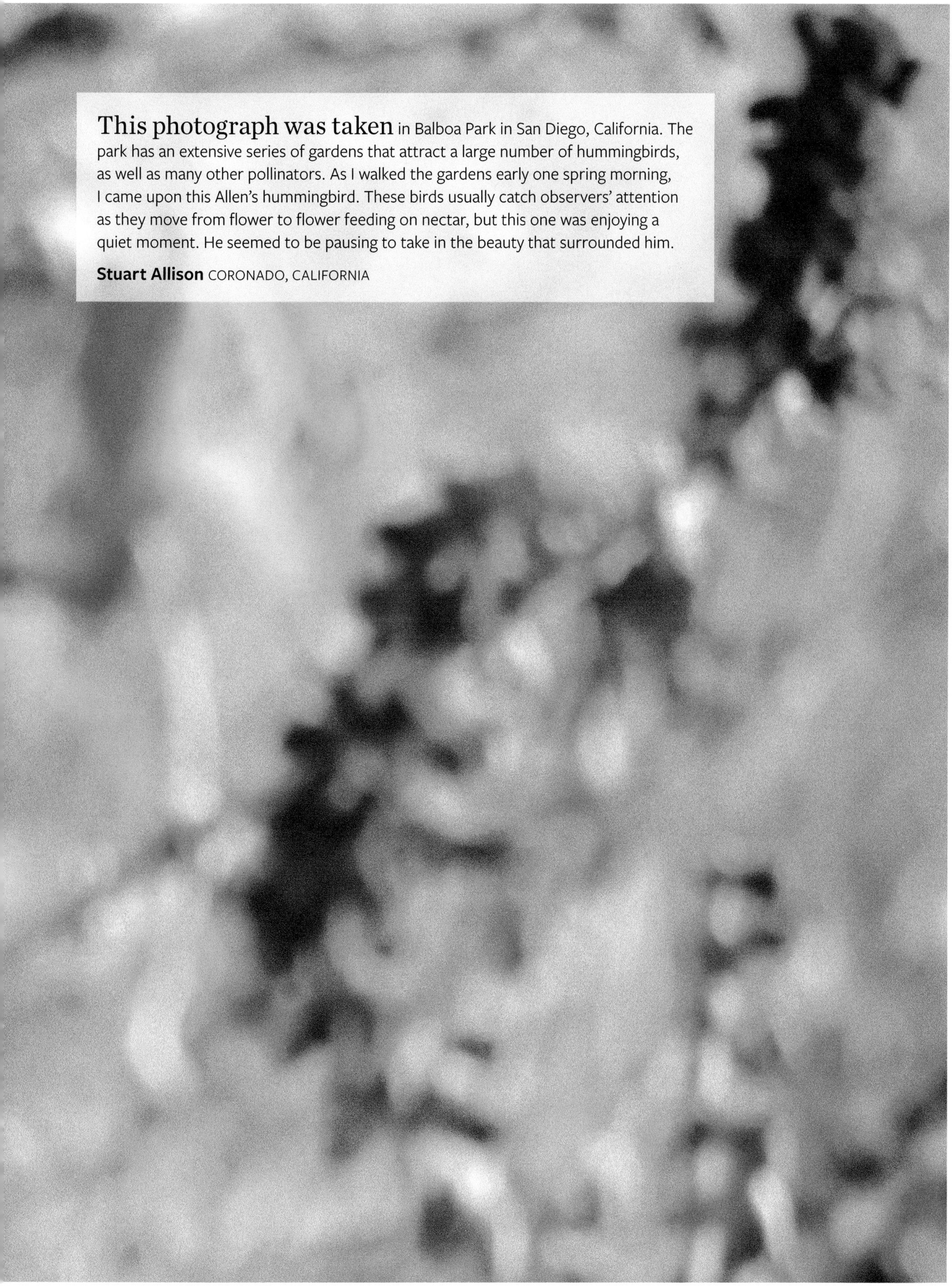

This photograph was taken in Balboa Park in San Diego, California. The park has an extensive series of gardens that attract a large number of hummingbirds, as well as many other pollinators. As I walked the gardens early one spring morning, I came upon this Allen's hummingbird. These birds usually catch observers' attention as they move from flower to flower feeding on nectar, but this one was enjoying a quiet moment. He seemed to be pausing to take in the beauty that surrounded him.

Stuart Allison CORONADO, CALIFORNIA

It's not often that I spot an owl in the wild, but on this particular morning, I saw two barred owls calling to each other and displaying. Here's one of them—it was such an amazing sight!

Laura Frazier KEARNEYSVILLE, WEST VIRGINIA

Blue grosbeaks are truly a breathtaking sight. One morning, I captured this brilliant male scanning his surroundings along an overgrown section of brush on the edge of a salt marsh—and saw dozens of other grosbeaks, too. I felt blessed to see such a strikingly beautiful bird.

Rick Hamilton
WESTMINSTER, MARYLAND

Recently the golf course just beyond my back fence was closed for extensive renovations. I went to the 11th green every day for two months to photograph a group of scissor-tailed flycatchers. They got to know me and didn't seem to mind me being there. This is one of my best shots.

Johnny Bliznak
ABILENE, TEXAS

TALL TAILS
To make sharp turns and stay agile, a scissor-tailed flycatcher relies on its elongated tail, which is longer than its body!

On my way

to Newport News Park in Newport News, Virginia, a light but steady rain began to fall. To protect my photo equipment from the rain, I wrapped both my Nikon camera and my lens in a plastic bag. I wasn't sure what kind of photos I'd captured, but while at the park, I caught sight of a male adult pileated woodpecker and two juveniles on a dead tree. The adult taught the youngsters how to get insects from the decaying bark. The young ones stayed at the base of the tree, while the adult hammered away above the ground, chips flying.

Richard Hogge
YORKTOWN, VIRGINIA

This photo was taken

at Devil's Lake State Park near Baraboo, Wisconsin. My family and I went hiking there one day and these geese decided to float right by us, one by one. It's probably not a rare sight, but it was the first time I had seen that many birds all lined up in a row. I think that they were playing follow the leader!

Andrea Brooks
HILL POINT, WISCONSIN

Every summer, I frequent a park near my home in Minneapolis that's been restored with native plants and flowers. As I admired this patch of smooth oxeye sunflowers, a chatty house wren flew in and perched right on one of the flowers. It was a fun opportunity for me to capture both a bird and a bloom in the same shot!

Travis Bonovsky BROOKLYN CENTER, MINNESOTA

COLORFUL TUNES

Only male painted buntings belt out songs—up to 10 per minute in spring as they establish their territorial boundaries singing *graffiti graffiti spaghetti-for-two.*

Painted buntings in West Texas are an all-time favorite for bird enthusiasts. I particularly love their gorgeous song and how they love to show it off. This photo shows how tenacious a singing painted bunting can be.

Tim Vasquez SAN ANGELO, TEXAS

I spotted this northern mockingbird

early one morning as it walked across a tree limb. I had my camera ready, and to my delight, it decided to take a big morning stretch. The photo reminds me of a bird photography tip: When all you have are common birds to photograph, try for uncommon shots. This was definitely one of those times!

Kimberly Miskiewicz
RALEIGH,
NORTH CAROLINA

Summer is very short

in Manitoba, but this photo definitely helps relieve the harshness of winter. It exudes the true excitement and color of summer.

Sujata Basu
WINNIPEG, MANITOBA

I grow tomatoes in containers on my deck, and one day I looked out to spy a juvenile red-bellied woodpecker enjoying one. I had no idea that woodpeckers would eat tomatoes!

Melissa Haggard
WINCHESTER, KENTUCKY

After several rainy days in a row, my wife noticed something moving in our backyard, which opens onto a wooded area. I slowly crept up and found a bird I had never seen before. Since that evening, this American woodcock has not revisited the yard.

Lawrence McCarty
SHAMONG, NEW JERSEY

It's a pleasure to spot brown-headed nuthatches

foraging among the pine needles and tree bark for seeds and insects. Very few birds use tools, but these nuthatches often search for insects by prying bark up from a tree using another piece of bark. They are active feeders, moving up, down and around trees very quickly, which means that photographing them can be quite a challenge. Just watching them always brings a smile to my face.

Michael Fitzgerald MERRITT ISLAND, FLORIDA

BRAINY BIRDS
A hummingbird's brain makes up around 4% of its body weight. It remembers every flower it visits!

Some of my best photos are taken right in my backyard. I plant perennials and annuals that specifically draw in the birds and bees. I love this action shot of a female ruby-throated hummingbird.

Jenny Miner IRMA, WISCONSIN

Indigo buntings

took up summer residence in the wooded area near my home. This male sang his clear and distinct song earnestly, sending notes over and through the trees. When he left, the females and juveniles remained here, feeding on berries and bugs until the young ones were old enough for their first-ever migration journey.

Liz Tabb
ELIZABETHTOWN, KENTUCKY

I love to photograph wildlife. Someone

told me about a local area that was home to a family of foxes, so I eagerly set up a blind to shoot from. I had no luck and was ready to take a break when something flew past my little window. I had no idea what it was but felt I ought to get some photos of it. It turns out that it was an immature chestnut-sided warbler! I'm so glad I didn't take that break.

Jim Knox
WILTON, MAINE

From my dining room

window, I noticed this ruby-throated hummingbird perched on a canna leaf near my oscillating sprinkler. Each time the spray came around, the bird flapped its wings and stretched toward the water. When the shower rotated away, the ruby-throat sat patiently, waiting. I'm glad I was inside, because I was able to watch the bird for several minutes unnoticed. I garden for these special moments!

Beverly Thevenin
CHESTERTON, INDIANA

My husband and I

turned our backyard into a haven for birds, bees and butterflies by planting flowers and trees that attract them. We've also put up bluebird houses. It was such a joy to watch a pair build a nest and care for their young. After their second brood left, three of the four young bluebirds returned to our backyard birdbath. I was outside and got a photo of them.

Deb Forster
CLAYTON,
NORTH CAROLINA

I've been photographing this osprey nest for the past four or five years. The same osprey couple returns each year to raise a few chicks, and this particular summer they successfully raised two. They were still adolescents when this photo was taken. The young one in front of the parent here was still unsure what to do with its wings.

Nancy Zimmerman CAPE MAY COURT HOUSE, NEW JERSEY

BEHIND THE NAME

Dickcissels earned their very unusual name thanks to the song they sing. If you're standing around in a prairie or many other tall grasslands, listen carefully for their *dick, dick, ciss, ciss ciss* call.

My husband and I visit nature centers during the summer, including Retzer Nature Center in Waukesha, Wisconsin. Walking along one of the pretty hiking trails, we heard an abundance of singing birds, including this male dickcissel. We also saw several bobolinks and American goldfinches that day.

Evelyn Johnson WAUWATOSA, WISCONSIN

A pair of sandhill cranes have been making their summer home on our property for the last few years. They have provided countless hours of enjoyment as we watch them preen, do their jumps and dances, and care for their colts. And their sound has to be heard to be believed!

Julie Heifort
ST. FRANCIS, MINNESOTA

I captured 30 photos of this beautiful female broad-tailed hummingbird as she sipped nectar from my Cold Hardy Pink salvia. I am blessed to see these flying jewels from about mid-July to the first week of October each year.

Linda Minns
GOODWELL, OKLAHOMA

I keep my camera in my living room near a window where I can open the screen. I love watching birds feed on our cherry tree. This photo of a red-bellied woodpecker is special to me because of the lighting, the colors of the bird and its pose as it reaches for its snack: a cherry.

Herbert Fields
WEST LAFAYETTE, INDIANA

This black-and-white warbler was a first-time visitor to my yard one summer, and it was such a delight to see. It has a beautiful song and a very different, striking look. Before gathering any information on the bird, I gave it the name zebra warbler.

Ginger English
BAUXITE, ARKANSAS

During a trip to Lake Thunderbird State Park here in Oklahoma, I got to see this beautiful snowy egret land on the water along the shoreline.

Stephen Ofsthun NORMAN, OKLAHOMA

This photo was taken the first time a pair of tree swallows chose to nest in one of our handmade boxes. We watched as both parents worked together to build the nest and gather food for their three babies. The adults took turns keeping guard on top of the box and hunting for insects. They didn't seem bothered by our presence and allowed us to get close while we weeded our nearby flower bed. Nature is beautiful, and this photo is a reminder for us all.

Tammy Hileman CELINA, OHIO

I was out checking cattle

when I came upon this common nighthawk. As I got closer, it kept a mindful eye on me, but let me take its picture anyway. Eventually, it became tired of being my photography subject and prepared itself for takeoff, which is when I captured this moment.

Stacy Ruder
WAKEENEY, KANSAS

This Rufous hummingbird

was guarding the feeder we had just put out and wouldn't let any other hummers come to it. But he sure was a joy to watch, with his brilliant orange gorget shining in the sunlight.

Deborah Whiting
MIDLAND, TEXAS

An American goldfinch duo flew down together and then landed on top of a mammoth sunflower. The muddled yellows of the female contrast with the bright gold of the male perched behind her. The female sang joyfully, and it almost seemed as though the pair had purposefully posed for me.

Bill Hoeflich
TRENTON, NEW JERSEY

The common loon is Minnesota's state bird. I've lived here all my life without ever seeing one until I visited my dad's lake cabin north of the Twin Cities. One of his neighbors offered to take me out on the lake to look for the resident loon. We eventually found it on the lake's other side. The sun was starting to set and the light beautifully reflected on the water.

Justin Pruden
ST. PAUL, MINNESOTA

BIRD ACROBATS
Downy woodpeckers have specialized feet that help them cling and climb.

Woodpeckers peck at tree trunks and suet feeders in my backyard. When I was visiting a botanical garden and heard the familiar tapping, I approached a tree to find a downy woodpecker. It flew by me and straight into a trumpet vine. I love how the red blossoms and green leaves create such a colorful backdrop.

Lucy Rogers ARLINGTON, TEXAS

It was my first time visiting South Texas to photograph the regional birds there. I sat patiently in a bird blind at Campos Viejos, near Rio Grande City. I was incredibly lucky to get a nice shot of a green jay in flight. (For the shutterbugs out there, I used a Nikon D5 with a 600mm lens.)

Diana Robinson PUNTA GORDA, FLORIDA

Near the end of June, I became aware of a strange sound coming from the woods behind our house. Through the Cornell Lab of Ornithology website, *allaboutbirds.org*, I learned the sound I was hearing belonged to fledgling barred owls begging for food. The next day, I located three young barred owls perched high in the trees along with an adult owl. Over the next several weeks, I found the owlets at various locations by listening for their begging calls.

Dorrie Holmes
GRANVILLE,
MASSACHUSETTS

On a beautiful sunny day in September, I was in my yard with my camera when I spotted a pretty yellow bird. I followed it through the leaves of the tree until it finally flew down to a small shrub. I couldn't believe that it had perched on a branch in plain view. It was a black-throated green warbler!

Keith Hopkin
SCARBOROUGH, ONTARIO

An eastern bluebird pair

had three eggs sitting in their nest when I took this photo. They chose to nest in the backyard of my friend's country home. She feeds these birds mealworms, and they patiently wait for their fill every morning.

Margie Whitling
ST. MARYS, OHIO

During a Fourth of July parade, a co-worker

noticed a hummingbird in its nest on a very low branch. With so many people sitting under it and walking nearby, we were amazed it did not fly off. We checked that nest every few days until the babies left. I call this shot *Full House*.

Deb DeCosta
HARWICH,
MASSACHUSETTS

My family and I visited Maine's Quoddy Head State Park on our vacation. During a two-hour hike around the park, we saw very few birds. We were starting to feel a little disappointed when, out of the blue, a beautiful grouse appeared! This spruce grouse, in full breeding plumage, wasn't even scared of us. In fact, he seemed to enjoy posing for the camera. Seeing this little male made the hike totally worth it.

Katie Muscatello SCHWENKSVILLE, PENNSYLVANIA

I took this photo of a reddish egret wading at Fort De Soto Park, close to St. Petersburg, Florida. For more than an hour, the egret energetically ran through the water and used the shade of its wings to reduce the glare as it speared fish. A storm was coming in off the gulf, and I had to pull myself away from this fascinating scene.

Ruth Skinner SEMINOLE, FLORIDA

A couple of years ago, a blue grosbeak visited my feeder for the first time. As I photographed him from the window, a cardinal landed to claim the feeder. They stared at each other for a couple of seconds before the grosbeak left and the cardinal got his spot back.

Beatriz Flores
HOUSTON, TEXAS

Every morning, I put an orange half at my feeder for this female Bullock's oriole that nested near my home. I got a big kick out of her pose! She stood like this multiple times, and I thought she was trying to tell the other birds that the orange was hers.

Dawn Key
ELIZABETH, COLORADO

I absolutely love all of the western scrub-jays that visit my backyard feeders! More than anything else, these birds can't resist peanuts in the shell. Many people find the jays noisy because of their harsh *shek-shek-shek* call, but I really like their blue markings and fun personalities.

Judy Albertson
TUALATIN, OREGON

I put oranges out for songbirds and was surprised to see the acorn woodpeckers enjoying them, too. The male on the right was eating by the time the female landed and took over. I had a whole acorn woodpecker family visiting my yard almost every day even though I don't have any oak trees nearby. Maybe the sweet orange treats have something to do with it!

Kitty Warner
MULE CREEK,
NEW MEXICO

ON THE MENU

From crickets and katydids to beetles and butterflies, if it's an insect, a great crested flycatcher probably eats it. Besides creepy crawlies, these birds eat small fruits and berries, but spit out the pit before swallowing them whole.

When I snapped this photo with my Nikon D800, this great crested flycatcher was living up to its name and catching flies. The bird and its mate were nesting in a wood duck house I'd put up by the pond in my backyard. I thought it was a beautiful bird in profile, and I like that this picture tells the story of its name.

B.J. Lanich WAUSAUKEE, WISCONSIN

Dickcissels prefer tall grassland habitat. The Neal Smith National Wildlife Refuge in Prairie City, Iowa, is one of the best spots to find them during the breeding season. A dickcissel's song is part of the sound of summer here in Iowa.

Douglas Lambert DES MOINES, IOWA

Although the red-eyed vireo is a common summer resident in Kentucky, it's a rare treat to actually spot one. This bird was in a wooded area near my home, munching on something yellow for its breakfast.

Liz Tabb
ELIZABETHTOWN,
KENTUCKY

Since I live in North Carolina, I see only ruby-throated hummingbirds. While I was on a vacation to southern Arizona, I was thrilled to capture this photo of a male broad-billed hummingbird.

Linda Jahn
HICKORY,
NORTH CAROLINA

One of my
favorite
birding and
photography hot spots
is South Llano River
State Park in Junction,
Texas. The park has four
marvelous bird blinds
with incredible diversity
at each one. Buntings
always create quite the
stir when they show
up. This year, bird-
watchers at the blinds
were especially thrilled
to see this bird, a very
rare hybrid between
a painted bunting and
varied bunting.

Cheryl Johnson
VICTORIA, TEXAS

Near my
parents'
home in northern
Pennsylvania is an open
field where a lot of
elderberry plants grow.
One year, I watched
10 species of warbler,
gray catbirds and cedar
waxwings dining on the
berries. And then to
my surprise, I saw this
black-billed cuckoo!
I was very excited, as
these birds are difficult
to see up close.

Joshua Galicki
WASHINGTON, D.C.

While at a local park, I noticed a lot of thistle. Once I knew it was there, I started to see goldfinches going crazy over the food source. They land on the plants, pick out the cotton-ball-like material and eat the seeds.

Kalley Cook LENOIR CITY, TENNESSEE

1. Ruby-throated at bee balm

8 Flowers Hummingbirds Love

Readers captured energetic birds zipping through their gardens. These nectar-rich blooms keep them buzzing back for more.

by Kirsten Schrader

1. Bee balm

Monarda, Zones 3 to 9
This plant fits the bill. It's vibrant, tube-shaped and full of nectar— everything a hummingbird wants. Plant bee balm in full sun and in well-draining soil. Then sit back and enjoy the fragrant flowers and the hummingbird show.

2. Zinnia

Zinnia, Annual
For a quick pop of color in the summer garden, sun-loving zinnias are a must. Plant a combination of single-bloom varieties in red and bright pink to make your yard more desirable to hummingbirds.

2. Ruby-throated at zinnia

3. Salvia

Salvia, Zones 4 to 11

Salvia is a hummingbird favorite because many other nectar seekers, such as bees and butterflies, are unable to access the nectar buried deep in the tubular blooms. That means more for the hummingbirds!

4. Alstroemeria

Alstroemeria, Zones 5 to 10

The vibrant, exotic look of this bulb is super attractive to hummingbirds. It's also a favorite of gardeners in the West.

5. Hosta

Hosta, Zones 3 to 8

Rising up to 3 feet above the foliage, hosta flowers are nectar-filled and dainty. The blooms last up to six weeks, so they are always at the ready whenever a hummingbird stops by.

3. Ruby-throated at salvia

4. Ruby-throated at alstroemeria

5. Ruby-throated
at hosta

6. Ruby-throated at crocosmia

6. Crocosmia

Crocosmia, Zones 5 to 9
Fiery red-orange blossoms burst to life in mid-to-late summer, offering your resident hummingbirds a sweet treat. For the best flowers, make sure to keep the soil moist.

7. Hibiscus

Hibiscus, Zones 4 to 9
This hardy favorite features flowers that span from 4 to 12 inches wide. It's a heat lover, so find a sunny spot and get ready to watch tiny birds visit the gigantic blooms.

8. Cape fuchsia

Phygelius, Zones 6 to 10
At 3 to 5 feet tall and wide, cape fuchsia commands attention in any garden, especially when the bright tube-shaped flowers are in bloom. A hummingbird's slender bill is a perfect fit!

7. Ruby-throated at hibiscus

Autumn Amazement

Discover stories about birds journeying to winter homes—
and those that stick around as the seasons change.

One cold day at the Minnesota Landscape Arboretum in the city of Chaska, Minnesota, I saw this female northern cardinal resting on a branch. She seemed to be looking over her shoulder with a light in her eye, and I love the way the edges of her feathers are lit up by the sun in this photo.

Roslynn Long BURNSVILLE, MINNESOTA

One morning a friend and I were hiking at the University of Guelph Arboretum in Ontario, Canada. We spotted this gorgeous leucistic white-throated sparrow. It was such a wonderful experience!

Brenda Doherty
ARISS, ONTARIO

WHITE AS SNOW

This sparrow isn't a true albino—it is leucistic. That means some or, in this case, most of its feathers lack pigment.

I spent a good hour or more on a small backwater pond with this spectacular great egret. I watched it successfully hunt a few small fish and then fly to the other side of the pond. I captured this image while it was flying. I used a long lens to keep my distance and let the bird go about its normal routine.

Eric Williamson
DES MOINES, IOWA

On a cold November day my husband came back from his walk and said he had been watching a pine grosbeak eat some berries back by the lake. I bundled up and, my camera tucked in my coat, trekked the half-mile out there, the whole time thinking the bird was probably long gone. But sure enough, there she was, a beautiful female grosbeak busily snacking on berries. As I crept closer, taking pictures, she remained totally oblivious. It was so funny watching her, especially when a berry got stuck on her bill and she tried hard to eat it.

Sue Ballreich
MARQUETTE, MICHIGAN

One gorgeous and bright

November afternoon, I heard a Carolina wren singing but couldn't locate it. Finding a spot where I could hide, I waited. Fortunately it was only a short time before this bird popped into view, singing away.

Dolan Trout
MONTGOMERY, ALABAMA

I stopped at the beautiful Ashokan Reservoir in New York with my wife and 4-month-old son. The scenery was fantastic even on a cloudy day. While we spent most of our time taking photos of foliage, we lucked out when we found this very cooperative bald eagle sitting in a pine tree along the walking path. It's the closest any of us have gotten to an eagle in the wild.

Phillip Werman NEW YORK, NEW YORK

White-eyed vireos were in my area all summer, and I saw several of them in a wooded area I visit often. This one cooperated with me on a sunny morning—it moved out of the shadows and made itself visible so I could take a picture. The elusive birds are hard to find, but a treat to hear!

Liz Tabb ELIZABETHTOWN, KENTUCKY

This lovely great horned owl must live in our neighborhood, since we've seen it quite a bit. I took this photo as the owl took a rest after chasing its prey across our backyard.

Bill Robertson
FORT COLLINS,
COLORADO

I took this photo at Ojibway Park in Windsor, Ontario. The little downy woodpecker is giving a northern cardinal a not-so-impressed look for stealing its seed.

Raven Ouellette
WINDSOR, ONTARIO

It was a gorgeous fall day, so my fiance and I decided to try capturing some of the season's vibrant colors. That's when we noticed a flock of golden-crowned kinglets eating aphids in a nearby maple tree. This particular bird took a moment to look for the source of the clicking sound before continuing his search for lunch.

Simon Valdez
BURNABY,
BRITISH COLUMBIA

I love how the visitors at my feeding station change with the seasons. Each year, I can't wait to see which birds show up as fall transitions to winter. This is one of the first house finches I spotted that year.

Ra Del Hinckley
INDEPENDENCE, MISSOURI

While I was checking out a small pond at Sedgwick County Zoo in Kansas, this male wood duck swam by. The fall colors from the surrounding trees were reflected in the water and made for some neat photos.

Suntesha Wustrack AUGUSTA, KANSAS

Northern mockingbirds seem to enjoy sitting on this euonymus shrub. I look for them in fall. When I took this photo, the striking backdrop was a crimson and orange maple tree. All the season's colors made the mockingbird seem so majestic.

Sujata Roy MORRISVILLE, NORTH CAROLINA

I was so excited to spot two pileated woodpeckers enjoying my suet feeder at the same time. I often see one woodpecker feeding here and there, but this was the first time I saw two at once.

Denise Brinkley
CROSSVILLE, TENNESSEE

SUET, SUET, SUET

Generally, woodpeckers' favorite feeder foods are suet, suet and suet! Offer it in cooler weather, when insects become very scarce.

Some people might say that cactus wrens lack the brilliant coloration of other bird species, but I love them. This image shows how well they can blend into their surroundings. I've been photographing birds for many years, and I've noticed that cactus wrens are quite social and tend to be one of the first birds that arrive on location, which was definitely the case when I photographed this one in a Tucson backyard.

Greg Tucker
LOS ANGELES,
CALIFORNIA

The intense glare of this Savannah sparrow makes it look very regal. I like the way the photo shows off the crisp outline of its feathers and the sharpness of its claws. Thanks to its simplicity, this photograph is one of my favorites.

Teresa Taylor
ST. MARYS, KANSAS

Early in fall

I came across this very handsome male spruce grouse hanging around an evergreen tree. I love the intricate patterns of the bird's feathers and always delight when I come across one.

Robin Edwards
HOMER, ALASKA

I was in the process of building a deck that overlooks this fountain when a Cooper's hawk flew in. When I saw it, I texted my wife and asked her to bring my camera outside, and to be very careful as she opened the sliding door. I was about 60 feet away from the hawk and noticed it seemed mesmerized by its reflection in the water bubble.

Stephen Smith AURORA, COLORADO

I was sitting quietly under a tree, trying to capture a picture of the common ground doves at Sonny Bono Salton Sea National Wildlife Refuge in California, but instead this cheeky male Gambel's quail strutted out in front of me. He looks so dapper with his fancy plume. I never thought a quail could be so cute!

Jodie Partin McNAUGHTON, WISCONSIN

I was baking pumpkin pies for our Thanksgiving feast when I caught this male eastern towhee looking at me. He jumped onto the ground underneath the feeders and found black oil sunflower seeds. I snapped this shot of him while he had his Thanksgiving meal.

Laurie Stuchlik
MILTON, DELAWARE

SCRITCH SCRATCH

Towhees spend quite a bit of their time kicking up dry leaves as they hunt for seeds and bugs to eat.

Short-eared owls migrate to the metro marshlands in Vancouver, British Columbia, each winter. They are often found hunting during the daytime but tend to be more active early in the morning and evening. One of my favorite experiences was when this owl landed about 30 to 40 feet away from me. I captured all of its great facial expressions.

Anthony Bucci
ABBOTSFORD,
BRITISH COLUMBIA

Fall is my favorite season in Michigan for many reasons, including the colors, apples and of course warblers. I spend quite a lot of time with my camera on the deck of our lake cottage in Covert, Michigan, hoping to spot a bright warbler. My patience was rewarded with this blackburnian warbler!

Megan Morrison
DEKALB, ILLINOIS

I waited out a late afternoon storm in hopes of having the opportunity to explore. After the downpour subsided, I captured this sweet broad-billed hummingbird finding the perfect perch on a beautiful agave plant. How lucky!

Joanna Proffitt
SURPRISE, ARIZONA

This yellow-shafted northern flicker showed off its lovely feathers in a tree near our deck, and I'm thankful I was looking outside at the right time to capture it. What an incredible beauty it is!

Ginny Phillips OLATHE, KANSAS

I was excited to visit a friend in Fort Myers Beach, Florida, especially because burrowing owls live nearby. But when we found them, we only saw their eyes. Finally, one owl came out. The look on its face when it saw me was priceless. It looked as if it was expecting to see another owl and was thinking, *Hey! You're not an owl!*

Sharon Panozzo BURBANK, ILLINOIS

When white-throated sparrows **return** to the Midwest, it's a signal that winter is on its way. Years ago, during the last warm week of the season in Indiana, I stumbled across a pair at my local park. I'd never seen these birds so close. Their yellow lores—the area between the eyes and the nostrils—are definitely my favorite.

Adam Wilson
GREENFIELD, INDIANA

I noticed many Steller's jays hanging around my songbird feeders. The jays liked the fruit and peanut mix in one, but it was too small for them to easily perch and eat. I picked up a hopper feeder and filled it with shelled peanuts. Now these beautiful birds with blue wings are regular visitors.

Phillip Lowe
PUYALLUP, WASHINGTON

SMART SINGERS

Steller's jays are intelligent mimics. They imitate birds, squirrels, cats, dogs, chickens and, occasionally, even mechanical objects.

Birds such as this sweet Carolina wren like stopping by the feeder that a friend made for me using a cup and saucer, chains, a spoon and some glass beads. The chain is cleverly attached to the saucer with three glued notebook clips. Several loops on the chain allow the feeder to be hung at various lengths. I love that the feeder is handmade, and it's fun to watch birds enjoying the seed there.

Mar Sension
ALTOONA, PENNSYLVANIA

The tufted titmouse's range doesn't extend far into my state. I was thrilled when I saw this one coming and going between my feeders and the nearby woods.

Patty Jennings
STACYVILLE, MAINE

GRAB AND GO

Titmice don't perch at feeders to eat seeds. They nab one, fly away to eat or stash it, then return.

Red-bellied woodpeckers are my favorite birds to see in the backyard. One summer, a male and female visited my feeders. Later on, I was delighted to see a new immature female show up. When late fall came, I still saw the male and sometimes the female.

Kathleen Janik OCONOMOWOC, WISCONSIN

The Dallas Arboretum always has a beautiful pumpkin display in October, and we visit every year to take pictures. A few years back, I was watching squirrels running around all the pumpkins when suddenly I heard a loud screech. As I turned around, I saw this male great-tailed grackle land right on a pumpkin. I really love this picture because the bird's black feathers are striking against the background of the orange pumpkins.

Michelle Christmas-Andrew DALLAS, TEXAS

This blue jay

was savoring the last of the crabapples left on this tree. It was only about 40 degrees outside, but the jay didn't seem to mind me taking its picture.

Rachel Fark
NEW BREMEN, OHIO

I was taking pictures

of the gorgeous fall foliage at my home in northern Minnesota when this amazing bald eagle landed near me, striking a pose as if just waiting to be photographed. I live on a lake where eagles nest every year, so they have become treasured neighbors. It's incredible to watch these majestic birds raise their new families. I never tire of watching them grab fish out of the lake and soar back to the nest to feed their fast-growing eaglets.

Debbie Center
NEVIS, MINNESOTA

This great horned owl lives in my yard, and I greatly enjoy watching and photographing both it and its sibling. This photo, taken on a windy afternoon, shows the 6-month-old owl trying to hang on to a branch of my sycamore tree.

Leslie Ashford
MADISON, MISSISSIPPI

I captured this photo at Middle Creek Wildlife Management Area, which is 20 minutes from my home. I love this shot because of the color and contrast—to me it looks as if this palm warbler posed for a painting.

Janet Zimmerman
LITITZ, PENNSYLVANIA

I was taking photos of some red-winged blackbirds when this female snatched up a dragonfly to feast on. Sometimes an opportunity like this one falls right into your lap, but other times you can shoot all day and not get many keepers. I took this photograph at a marsh connected to Lake George in New York.

Don Blais MECHANICVILLE, NEW YORK

Whenever I spend an early morning walking through my local park, I usually see a hawk soaring past, looking for something to eat. On this particular morning a male and female red-shouldered hawk were flying around, and they both landed on a nearby tree. I just so happened to have my camera with me, and was thrilled I could get this picture.

Alice Beaman BRAZIL, INDIANA

There's a nice quiet spot in a little village in Ontario called Port Bruce. I love to spend a few days there in the fall, watching the warblers migrate. On this day, a beautiful Nashville warbler made an appearance.

Trisha Snider
ST. THOMAS, ONTARIO

FAMOUS EYE RING

A Nashville warbler's most distinctive marking is its white eye ring. Also look for a gray head and a striking yellow throat and chest.

This blue jay

had been eluding me all summer, but I was finally in the right place at the right time. I snapped this photograph in my backyard last fall.

Bonnie Schnabl
SULLIVAN, WISCONSIN

My backyard is one of my favorite places to watch nature. I was keeping an eye out for visiting deer when I saw movement in the trees. This stunning barred owl caught my attention, and I thought it looked as if it was posing for its portrait.

Wanda Donihoo
JULIETTE, GEORGIA

It was truly a beautiful fall day, but I was a little sad because I knew that soon all the hummingbirds would be flying south for the winter. This cute young hummer cheered me up by posing for the camera. It put on quite a show and let me snap shot after shot.

April McCormack
FULTON, KENTUCKY

BIG APPETITES
Before migrating, hummingbirds may increase their body weight by more than 50%.

We are fortunate to have an adorable sandhill crane family of three frequent our property. I love observing and photographing such exquisite and beautiful creatures. I recently captured this special moment between the juvenile crane and one of its parents.

Renee Blake FENTON, MICHIGAN

This pileated woodpecker landed on a stump near my home and immediately began searching for food. A close look at its beak shows a small insect it found. I was glad I had my Nikon D300 with me so I could get the shot before the woodpecker took off. A friend witnessed the scene and could not believe the bird landed so close to me.

Tom Lusk LANSDOWNE, ONTARIO

It was a cold, rainy day when a ring-necked pheasant first came into our yard. It didn't appear to be healthy, but its presence still made us happy. We fed him for a few months, watching him grow and his feathers develop more detail. He lived in the shrubs in our yard, which is strange because we live in the city. He was there for a while until he left in spring. Whenever we spot a ring-necked, we always wonder if it is "our pheasant."

Blake Giddings
XENIA, OHIO

It's always a thrill to capture blue jays showing their dominant personalities. They bicker when I put out food, but there's plenty for everyone!

Jacqueline Hodsdon
FOREST, VIRGINIA

I have turned my backyard into a bird sanctuary with goldfinch feeders, hummingbird feeders, a birdbath—you name it! Never in my wildest dreams did I believe I would attract such a large variety of birds, though. Bushtits, black phoebes, Nuttall's woodpeckers, orange-crowned warblers and Anna's hummingbirds have all stopped by. But the one bird I really can't get enough of is the yellow-rumped warbler. It doesn't come around often and is very shy and difficult to photograph. I was very lucky to have gotten this photo of it.

Sheralyn Maddock
RANCHO PALOS VERDES, CALIFORNIA

Some might think black-capped chickadees are boring birds, but I think of them as a true force of nature. They are persistent, and I find them smart and charming. This one landed on a branch as I was waiting for the perfect moment to try to capture its spunk.

Kaitlyn Grib
RICHMOND, MAINE

This photo was taken along a pathway near our home in North Pole, Alaska. The great horned owl appeared to be hunting. At the time, it was a very quiet fall evening, and no other birds were stirring in the woods.

Laurie Gerber NORTH POLE, ALASKA

Ruby-crowned kinglets normally move constantly, but this one stayed still just long enough for me to photograph it against the soft orange background. It was November, and the colors of my favorite season really show!

Laura Frazier KEARNEYSVILLE, WEST VIRGINIA

Every fall and winter, I watch for the returning gray catbirds as they migrate back to Florida for some warm weather and food. An easy way to attract catbirds is to grow a berry-producing plant, like this beautyberry.

Peter Brannon
TAMPA, FLORIDA

Although I've seen many downy woodpeckers, I was so happy to spot my first hairy woodpecker while it dined on the berries of this poison ivy vine. It was perfect timing. The bold black-and-white of the hairy contrasted with the orange leaves, as if it knew Halloween was around the corner.

Liz Tabb
ELIZABETHTOWN, KENTUCKY

SPOT THE DIFFERENCE
Snowy egrets have black bills and are smaller than yellow-billed great egrets.

One morning, I was watching this snowy egret search for food in Mobile Bay, Alabama. The bird used its foot to stir up the ground, but looked amusingly frustrated and ruffled while doing it. But one of the reasons this photo came out so well is because of the amazing lighting, which was due, in part, to the cool, crisp air.

Benjamin Cash LOXLEY, ALABAMA

While picking out pumpkins, I saw some broom corn and opted to hang it up near my backyard feeders. The American goldfinches, which had been absent for about a month, quickly came back to eat the seeds and use the broom corn as a perch while waiting around for the feeders. It certainly made for a beautiful photograph.

James Prutilpac MORGANTOWN, WEST VIRGINIA

I was lucky enough to watch this beautiful eastern phoebe one day. The bird came close and gave me many different poses. It was the first time I'd ever seen this type of bird.

Kathy Wooding
HIGHLAND PARK,
NEW JERSEY

THE FIRST BANDED BIRD

John James Audubon himself tied thread to an eastern phoebe's leg to track its migration in 1804.

The birds seemed to be waiting for my husband and me. As soon as we came home, they flocked to the feeders. As I snapped a few photos, this American tree sparrow looked right at me as if it was thinking, *It's about time you got home! I'm starving!* My favorite thing about this species is their gray bushy eyebrows, which remind me of a grandfather's. I call these cute birds "old man sparrows."

Susan LoParco
CORTLAND, NEW YORK

During a hike, we found a family of loons swimming under a bridge. The shallow water was so clear that we could see the parents teaching their two babies how to dive for fish. The patterns on their backs were quite dazzling.

Lisa Howard
ST. PAUL, MINNESOTA

Every autumn I look forward to the annual migration of the sandhill cranes through southeastern Tennessee. Most years, it's October when I hear the distinct throaty call of cranes flying overhead. The weary travelers rest for a couple of months at the Hiwassee Wildlife Refuge near Birchwood, Tennessee, where I photographed these three birds in flight.

Dan Sommers
CHATTANOOGA,
TENNESSEE

NOT EASILY FOUND
While yellow- and black-billed cuckoos are fairly common in their ranges, they're quite elusive and easily overlooked.

It was quite a treat to photograph this yellow-billed cuckoo, since I've seen only one other in my six years as a birder. It was sitting in a wild persimmon tree near my home on the Eastern Shore.

Nancy Wyman CHESTERTOWN, MARYLAND

I was photographing two young mule deer when a western scrub-jay landed on a branch next to one of them. After a few moments, the jay hopped onto the deer's back, flitted in place a few times, then landed on the deer's head! The doe calmly let the jay hunt for fleas and ticks. When the bird was finished grooming the first deer, it flew to the second one's head and proceeded to comb it for bugs. I've seen photos of this, but I had never seen it in nature.

Vicki Miller KELSEYVILLE, CALIFORNIA

Red Rocks Park in Denver

is mostly known for its outdoor amphitheater, which draws big-name entertainers. But it also has also a small area where feeders offer seed for birds during the colder months. I spotted this lovely dark-eyed junco atop the retaining wall in the morning sun.

Carl Muehlemeyer
BROOMFIELD, COLORADO

While visiting a friend in the town

of Florence, Arizona, I spotted two burrowing owls. At first I thought they were a couple of lumps of dirt, until one did some lovely posing for me. But this one hung back for the longest time. When it finally decided to pop up, it just stood there with this deer-in-the-headlights stare. I told my friend all about her amusing owl neighbors; now she texts me from time to time when she spots them.

Pat Schoenfelder
IMPERIAL, NEBRASKA

Red-bellied woodpeckers come to my feeder for sunflower seeds. They prepare for winter by grabbing a seed, and then stashing it in the trees in my yard to eat later. It's so fun to watch this behavior.

Rebecca Granger
BANCROFT, MICHIGAN

After the first cold front of the year, I headed to a local lake for some birding. Most birds stayed sheltered in the underbrush, but eventually my patience paid off. A mixed flock moved toward a yaupon bush full of red berries, and after a few minutes, a ruby-crowned kinglet gave me this picture-perfect shot.

Ron Newhouse
BRYAN, TEXAS

NOT SO FAR SOUTH

Most warblers fly to the tropics for winter but some, such as the yellow-rumped, stay in the southern United States.

This yellow-rumped warbler came to eat a ripening persimmon one recent October. The bird has been an autumn visitor to our Southern California yard for the last several years. I've also spotted it eating suet in the winter.

James Tucker VENTURA, CALIFORNIA

It's the loud squawking from above that lets me know the sandhill cranes have arrived in Albuquerque each fall. I captured these two slowly strolling through the tall grass seconds before they took flight.

Karen Jones RIO RANCHO, NEW MEXICO

I had often watched geese and mallards at nearby Evergreen Lake, but I'd never heard of a wood duck before. So when a friend mentioned seeing wood ducks at Sterne Park in Littleton, I was curious. We came upon the colorful birds swimming in the park's pond. What a lovely fall afternoon it was!

Ann Zimmerman
IDAHO SPRINGS,
COLORADO

I truly love photographing small birds when their rapid movement and the trees' interfering branches add to the challenge of getting a standout shot. I'm red-green colorblind, so the way this pine warbler flitted about attracted me. If it had been a painted bunting or a cardinal, I might not have even noticed it! The pine warbler seemed curious about my camera, and it paused long enough for me to get this picture.

Mark Menser
WINDER, GEORGIA

The sun was setting as this female northern cardinal perched on a branch, waiting for her turn at the feeder. The warm light from the sun hitting her feathers made her look all the more beautiful and eye-catching.

Carolyn Stuart
KANNAPOLIS,
NORTH CAROLINA

Bird-watching has always been one of my favorite hobbies. I was playing around with a camera in my front yard when I saw this female house finch fly overhead and land on a branch not too far from me. I kept sneaking closer to her and took this picture. I love the red fall leaves of the tree she landed on!

Karlie Larson
SPIRIT LAKE, IDAHO

LISTEN AND LOOK

When pileated woodpeckers are nearby, you will hear the *wuk wuk* calls of these vocal birds long before you are able to spy one.

After offering suet for years, I finally attracted pileated woodpeckers. I was out with my camera when a male landed. While I was taking his picture, he called for his mate. Sure enough, after about 10 minutes, this female flew in.

Nancy Roberts JERSEY SHORE, PENNSYLVANIA

A pumpkin doubles as a feeder and a fall photo op for this downy woodpecker.

Host a Peanut Party

Jays, woodpeckers and chickadees, guaranteed! They may bring along some of their friends— tanagers, robins and wrens.

by Sally Roth

t's true. Birds go nuts for the fat- and protein-packed treat that is super easy for backyard bird-watchers to serve. Peanuts in almost any form are a lifesaver in the depths of winter, but they will draw a huge crowd year-round.

"Don't underestimate the attractiveness of peanuts in the shell," says Scott Edwards, guest editor of the National Bird-Feeding Society. "Blue jays seem to prefer them this way, and woodpeckers, chickadees and titmice will take them on as well." Peanuts in the shell tempt cardinals, chickadees, mockingbirds and more. Serve them chopped and birds that typically eat soft foods, such as tanagers, wrens, bluebirds and thrashers, will come to the peanut feast.

Raw or roasted? It's a common question, and birds love both, but "we generally recommend against salted peanuts," says Holly Faulkner, project assistant for Project FeederWatch at the Cornell Lab of Ornithology.

Put out the peanut feeders, and let the bird circus begin!

Jays

If you've ever attempted to grab a big handful of potato chips, you'll laugh when you watch jays try to do the same with peanuts. Discarding those that don't fit, they stuff as many as possible into their throat pouch and bill. All blue-colored jay species are enthusiastic peanut eaters—and also stashers, caching their treasures under tree bark, in

This blue jay is likely going to stash its peanut away to eat it later.

All five of the North American titmice—tufted, black-crested, juniper, bridled and oak—stop by feeders for a peanut snack.

Peanuts in almost any form are attractive to birds. Just be sure you set out the unsalted kind.

crevices or beside rocks to go back and retrieve later.

Woodpeckers
Every woodpecker, from the adorable downy to the giant pileated, eagerly snatches peanuts to eat on the spot or store for a later date. Whole, chopped or shelled—when it comes to these snacks, they are not picky.

Small songbirds
Chickadees, titmice and nuthatches may be small, but they're among the biggest peanut fans. Songbirds are known to hammer the shell, holding it down with their feet. They carry off shelled nuts to stash or eat elsewhere, and they also eagerly devour chopped ones. All of these

little gray birds usually take their treats to go, but you can bet they will come back again and again.

Northern cardinals
Serve these beauties peanuts out of the shell as whole or half nuts, or chopped. The pyrrhuloxia, the "desert cardinal" of the Southwest, loves this food just as much as its bright red relative.

Wrens
These perky-tailed birds favor shelled or chopped peanuts. If the nuts aren't chopped, wrens work hard to break off manageable bits. Any species of wren in the neighborhood may visit a peanut feeder, and once a bird finds it, it'll soon be a regular.

Native sparrows, juncos, towhees and doves
Keep an eye on the ground beneath peanut feeders, where you'll find white-throated, white-crowned, golden-crowned, song and other native sparrows, along with juncos, towhees and doves, gathered to peck up bits that other birds dropped.

Surprise guests
Bluebirds, robins, crossbills and other uncommon feeder birds might visit peanut feeders. "Catbirds, orioles and tanagers happily consume the broken-off pieces from birds pecking the larger nuts," Scott says. So will thrashers, robins, mockingbirds, bluebirds, and birds that usually eat insects, fruit and other soft foods.

A female northern cardinal makes friends with a frog at this peanut feeder.

Let it Snow

In a bright, wintry world, birds enduring the chilly
weather entertain and delight photographers.

EARLY DINNER
Black rosy-finches stop by feeders in the western mountains. Fill feeders in the late afternoon to give birds energy before chilly winter nights.

On the last day of our trip to the Southwest, we stopped at Sandia Crest in New Mexico. Frost covered the landscape and birds swarmed the feeding station. A black rosy-finch landed in front of us, perching on a perfectly frosted branch. I took the shot just as the sun came out from the clouds. It was an ideal end to an amazing trip to the Southwest!

Martina Nordstrand INDIAN TRAIL, NORTH CAROLINA

It was a bitterly cold day when this ring-necked pheasant decided to perch on my railing. It showed up every now and then, fluffing its plumage to stay warm. The pheasant wasn't very fearful, so I was able to capture this shot. It's an excellent example of the rainbow of colors pheasants display.

John Perlberg
MORO, WISCONSIN

As soon as the sun was up, I was hoping to snatch a few photos of birds in the bright, fresh snow. Imagine my delight when this yellow-rumped warbler stopped near me! It stayed around for much longer than I expected, allowing me to get this shot. It's as if the wintry warbler knew how the pale blue sky and white snow complemented its yellow patches.

Kimberly Miskiewicz
RALEIGH,
NORTH CAROLINA

At this time of year, we think of decorating and hanging ornaments on our lovely Christmas tree. I also love to look outside and see nature's winter ornaments, such as red berries encased in ice, which are stunning against a winter background. But nothing brightens a scene like a male cardinal in the snow.

Anne Duvall
GREENCASTLE, PENNSYLVANIA

This tiny common redpoll was patiently waiting for his turn at a feeder in my backyard on a cold morning when I noticed him. I know winter must be a hard time of year for birds, so I keep my feeders filled.

Jim Van Schyndel
PULASKI, WISCONSIN

I never leave home without my camera. I pulled over one day to capture some birds in a tree. Then I saw this darling pair of California quails snuggling on a fence post in the snow. I was so excited!

Kim Steed MINDEN, NEVADA

In Cincinnati, Ohio, we have a street called Wentworth that is lined with rows of hawthorn trees. Every winter, tons of robins gather to eat the berries. After a bad snow and ice storm a couple of years ago, I came across this robin sitting on an icy branch.

Laura Retyi CINCINNATI, OHIO

Some days, the winter skies are drab and full of clouds. Yet it's on those dark days that mellow colors become rich, especially when there is no light to cause contrast, as happens on sunny days. One dark day, this American tree sparrow momentarily perched on a fir branch. I set my camera to an aperture that allowed for a lot of light to enter, so it blurred out the background. I think the image has the feel of a painting.

Laurie Dirkx
ONTARIO, NEW YORK

Following an ice storm, I ventured into the yard with my camera to photograph the ice formations on the trees and came upon a lone male bluebird. As I snapped a few pictures, another bluebird flew in to join him—and, not long after, a third came along. They huddled together for a long time, letting me get very close. They looked as eager for spring to arrive as I was! This picture is my favorite.

Diane Johnston
ATOKA, TENNESSEE

An intense mind game

occurred when this barred owl tried to snag a red squirrel. I looked on as the squirrel and owl watched each other. The owl was so intent on pursuing its prey that it looked at me only once! It lost the game, though, and the squirrel got away.

Jim Knox
WILTON, MAINE

I love when it

snows here in Seattle because it's so much easier to see varied thrushes. They like to come up to my deck and tree out front.

Kirk Gibbs
FEDERAL WAY,
WASHINGTON

MIGRATION MYSTERY
Researchers have been mystified for decades about when and why some blue jays migrate and others don't. Some stay in the same region all year; others migrate one year and not the next.

One winter brought brutal below-zero temperatures. I took photos through the window and occasionally threw out peanuts for the blue jays. They sat in the tree watching me and waiting for the treat. Birds do make winter more pleasant!

JoAnne Pionessa WARSAW, NEW YORK

This decorative birdhouse in our yard was vacant for more than 10 years before a male red-shafted flicker claimed it. The main entrance was far too small for him, so for several weeks we had the pleasure of watching him remodel. Finally, at dusk one day, I saw him scoot through his brand-new front door. We call the house his bachelor pad, because when the female or juveniles get near the roof, he sends them away. He seems to take a summer vacation, but for most of the winter, as dusk settles, we can hear his call. If the coast is clear, he ducks inside!

Cindy Haubert LONGMONT, COLORADO

Pheasant populations in central Illinois are dismal. Habitat, weather and predators have taken a toll on these beautiful birds. Imagine my surprise when I went out for a Christmas Day photography trip and discovered this very stunning male not far from my home!

Amanda Fox
WOODSON, ILLINOIS

About a dozen robins frolicked as the snow fell, and, despite the risk to my equipment, I had to get some pictures. The birds didn't seem to mind that I was right under their tree, balancing an umbrella on my head while trying not to get my camera wet! This little robin just sat on its branch, watching me so intently that it let a few flakes pile up on its head.

Jeri Stunkard
WESTMINSTER,
COLORADO

Sometimes the weather makes it difficult to go to your favorite places and capture all the beauty of winter. But it's always fun to decorate your backyard so feathered visitors can come to you. This red-breasted nuthatch was a regular visitor to our feeders. I put a few treats in the pot and it became a sweet place for the bird to come sit for a bit and enjoy the December sun's warmth.

Sharon Sauriol
WASHINGTON, MICHIGAN

On an extremely cold winter day in Wisconsin, several cardinals and other birds visited my feeders. I have always dreamed of seeing special birds with unique features, and that day I did. I wasn't sure about the proper name for this leucistic cardinal, so at the time I called it "white head." It's such a beauty!

Barb Wood
RICHLAND CENTER, WISCONSIN

I frequent the trails at Proud Lake Recreation Area in Michigan, and one winter day I saw a large bird fly into a tree. I initially thought it was a hawk, only to be stunned when I got closer and saw it was a barred owl. It was my first experience with one of these owls, though since then I've encountered many at the park.

Shawn Spencer COMMERCE TOWNSHIP, MICHIGAN

After a round of icy weather overnight, I snapped a close-up of this eastern towhee. I think it was happy to stop by for some breakfast!

Danna Cable STATESVILLE, NORTH CAROLINA

A juvenile Cooper's hawk had been hanging around our backyard for a few weeks, always just out of reach of my camera. As luck would have it, the hawk happened to perch outside our bedroom window when the light was just right. I was able to capture this very pretty moment.

Dave Lyman
KALAMAZOO, MICHIGAN

Our blue jays can't get enough peanuts. I made a trip outside to fill the feeder and I had a few left over, so I placed them on the rail of our gazebo. Back inside, before I even got my jacket off, I looked out the window and saw a jay with a peanut in its mouth.

Darla Stocker
TIPTON, INDIANA

On the very last day of our trip in Meadowlands, Minnesota, near Sax-Zim Bog, we saw five great gray owls within three hours and this was one of them. (We'd spent all week looking for owls and other boreal birds.) I liked how the falling snow added a touch of magic as the great gray owl flew near the roadside. It really gives you a sense of the bone-chilling winters these owls have to survive.

Jessica Botzan
VANDERGRIFT,
PENNSYLVANIA

It was a bitterly cold winter, but for the first time, we had eastern bluebirds in our yard. After they got a drink from the heated birdbath, they flew over to one of our trees. Initially they were spread out across the branch, but inch by inch they shuffled toward one another until they were huddled together for warmth.

Steve Trupiano
O'FALLON, MISSOURI

FAVORITE FOODS

Unlike the majority of bird species, cedar waxwings are able to survive on a diet of berries alone for months if necessary.

I still find the adult cedar waxwing to be one of the most beautiful birds around, even after photographing birds for more than 40 years. Every time I see one up close it looks surreal, as though it was just painted. I continue pursuing these magnificent birds and never get tired of photographing them.

Willy Onarheim MEDFORD, OREGON

It was lightly snowing. I had just put out my peanut butter log
to help the birds get through an unusually cold winter when this hairy woodpecker
arrived. I grabbed my camera to photograph it when suddenly a noisy blue jay flew
in and landed right on top of the log. The jay didn't see the woodpecker, which
quickly ran up from the bottom of the log and confronted the blue jay. The jay
was startled and reared back. The two of them stood their ground for a while, but
eventually the woodpecker scared the jay off to a nearby weeping cherry tree.

Sandra Yahn-Wise AUBURN, NEW YORK

In midwinter, pine siskins were eating us out of house and home. This one patiently waited at the feeder, which was pretty unusual for them in those days!

Kathryn Kauth
GREEN BAY, WISCONSIN

On my way to work, I walk past a restaurant. One day, I noticed a group of Anna's hummingbirds buzzing around, and I captured several photos, including one of this bright male posing among the eatery's cheery Christmas lights.

Rick Kleinosky
CORVALLIS, OREGON

Several years ago, I made a special trip to Davenport, Iowa, just to photograph the bald eagles on the Mississippi River. Watching them fish and seeing the skill they displayed was an absolutely amazing experience. I highly recommend it!

Mike Dickie
ADRIAN, MICHIGAN

I put a bird feeder on a shepherd's hook right outside my kitchen window, near the cherry tree, so I could photograph birds as close to the window as possible. I ended up with 17 evening grosbeaks that flew into my yard for their dinner. This is just one of many photos I took of these pretty golden birds; this one seems to be making sure I get his good side.

Laurie Painter
SILVER CLIFF, WISCONSIN

THE RIGHT HABITAT

Sandhill cranes seek open areas, so if you live near fields or marshes, you might see a sandhill venture into your yard!

We are so fortunate that beautiful sandhill cranes visit us regularly, returning in late spring to nap under our birch trees and nibble from our feeders. This lovely bird thrilled me with its early arrival, even staying in place while I ran for my camera. I love the way its red mask stands out against the snowy background.

Renee Blake FENTON, MICHIGAN

On a cold, gloomy winter day, I was driving through a particularly boggy area in Minnesota, just hoping I would see something I could photograph. Before I knew it, I came across a majestic great gray owl! It stared me down as I snapped this photo.

Paul Danaher CHICAGO HEIGHTS, ILLINOIS

Right outside our back window we have a variety of trees and shrubs that the birds love to use as shelter from the elements. It's also the perfect photography setup. Cardinals are among my favorites to photograph in winter because of the contrast their feathers create with the falling snow.

Noelle Sippel
WEBSTER, NEW YORK

The day after a huge snowstorm, all of the birds came out from their hideaways. I noticed a large flock of bushtits darting through the trees, so I grabbed my camera in case one of them sat still for a second. I was grateful for the opportunity to photograph a bird that is common in Colorado but difficult to capture!

Russell Pickering
LOVELAND, COLORADO

BELOVED BIRDS

The American goldfinch is so cherished that it is the state bird of three states. Depending where you are, you might hear them referred to as willow or eastern goldfinches.

I was at the Lowry Nature Center

in Victoria, Minnesota, on a cold winter day. I was watching for birds at the top of a hill in the gently falling snow. The area had a lot of dry plants, and this goldfinch landed on a stem near me. I loved the way the snow and distant grasses created a soft scene. The goldfinch was holding on to the stem in such a delicate way.

Roslynn Long BURNSVILLE, MINNESOTA

The snow was softly falling when this tufted titmouse came in to feed one early winter morning. It sat on the branch, feathers fluffed to keep warm. This photo is one of my favorites.

Rebecca Granger
BANCROFT, MICHIGAN

We had our bird feeder up for just a few days, and we quickly acquired some regular visitors. This red-bellied woodpecker was my favorite, not only for its dazzling markings, but also for its amusing personality. It couldn't seem to decide if it wanted to eat the seeds from the feeder or make a home out of our deck railing.

Brianna Rob
KARNS CITY,
PENNSYLVANIA

Birds begin to migrate through our area in summer and fall, and Cooper's and sharp-shinned hawks frequently visit our yard to "play" with the blue jays. This sharp-shinned stopped by one rainy day and parked on a tree in our yard. His posture in this picture reminds me of a magician. I can just imagine him thinking, *And for my next trick...*

Don Whitehead DULUTH, MINNESOTA

Bohemian waxwings are my favorite winter birds. Oftentimes, a few of my photographer friends and I bundle up and go out together in search of them. I look forward to their cheerful arrival again ever year.

Amy Bragg ANCHORAGE, ALASKA

Here's a very special snowy owl that visited our area and stayed for a month or so. The owl originally perched on the roof of a building, looking for lunch. As she flew away, we walked back to the car and found she was right around the corner of the building, behind a fence. We all stopped in our track and took a few shots, and off she went again. It was an amazing experience.

Elaine Hessler
AVON, OHIO

We thought winter was finally done for the year, but yet another blast of snow came. I ventured out with my trusty Nikon camera to one of my favorite spots. This red-shafted northern flicker's movements were quick as he made his rounds between the mountain ash berries and crabapples.

Meghann Fletcher
PENTICTON,
BRITISH COLUMBIA

The evening grosbeak is one of the most dramatic winter finches to come from Canada to northeastern Minnesota's coniferous forests. These colorful grosbeaks are a favorite at my feeders. Large flocks of them can be seen at the Sax-Zim Bog, which is north and west of Duluth. This species seems to have spread eastward about a century ago as box elder trees and other winter food sources became more plentiful.

Donald Kaddatz
MORA, MINNESOTA

An Anna's hummingbird spends winters in my yard. One day, I sat at the window waiting for the bird to light on the snow-covered butterfly bush. Eventually, the beautiful winter jewel obliged.

Kristi Gruel
SNOHOMISH, WASHINGTON

This is one of my favorite photographs of a yellow-rumped warbler. It was winter and no leaves were on my trees. The bird hopped from branch to branch, posing for me before it flew away.

Betsy Moseley ZELLWOOD, FLORIDA

It looks as if this house finch is taking a shower under a dried-up sunflower as it whips up snow with its wings.

Norma Larrabee Gabriel MENOMONIE, WISCONSIN

Brilliantly colored blue jays are some of my favorite winter birds. This particular one looks as if it's trying to show off. It seems to be thinking, *I'm going to pretend I don't see you taking my picture, but here's my good side.*

Noelle Sippel
WEBSTER, NEW YORK

We came across this ruffed grouse near a fallen tree just off the road. A recent snowfall lent a picturesque background to the wintry scene. The grouse allowed me to approach within a few feet to get this gorgeous picture.

Lori Dyer
MOORHEAD, MINNESOTA

I am honored to be a volunteer at Blackwater National Wildlife Refuge in Cambridge, Maryland. This comes with the opportunity to get photos of our migrating birds when they stop to refuel for their travels. These are just a couple of snow geese out of the thousands that visit us every winter, from December to March.

Beverly Middleton
EAST NEW MARKET, MARYLAND

This gorgeous Steller's jay

lives near my mountain cabin. Whenever I show up, I always bring a bag of peanuts. All I have to do is whistle and the birds come to eat! I'm always excited and entertained as I watch them fly in and out.

Bobbie Rash
HELENA, MONTANA

One day this northern mockingbird visited our winterberry shrub while it was snowing. It is an uncommon sight for us. I was thrilled to capture this beautiful moment and bird.

George Kurzik HELLAM, PENNSYLVANIA

Traffic at the feeder was uncharacteristically quiet, with the exception of a few noisy crows expressing their displeasure with this barred owl visitor. The owl was as unfazed by the crows' rude calls as it was by the snow piling up on its head. It perched by the feeder for the entire morning and into the afternoon.

Connie Bocko WATERVILLE, NEW YORK

Mountain bluebirds venture to the plains whenever late-season snows arrive. This bird was part of a flock devouring juniper berries while escaping the chill of the Rocky Mountains. The bluebirds stayed in the area for several days, until all the berries were gone.

Neal Zaun
BOULDER, COLORADO

This wasn't a normal day with my camera. Just about every male and female cardinal from the surrounding area came in to feed after a harsh blizzard. My fence is usually popular with neighborhood birds waiting their turn to eat, but this was a very special moment.

Carol Estes
LA PORTE, INDIANA

A rare Mississippi snow blew through our area, and this common grackle paused to pout right outside our kitchen window. His expression reminds me of an Angry Birds character. I imagine him thinking, *I chose to live in Mississippi for a reason! What's up with all this white stuff falling from the sky?*

Teri Metts
MENDENHALL, MISSISSIPPI

Flurries had just started to fall. It was a nice, gentle snow, perfect for photos. These goldfinches cozied up while they waited for a turn at my feeder.

Lisa Hostetter
WAVERLY, MISSOURI

Once, in early spring, I let my dog out and saw a flash of white. Knowing there aren't any white birds in this area of Minnesota, I decided to investigate. On closer inspection, it looked like a partially albino male robin. Instead of flying off, he stuck around for over a week, sitting in the treetops and singing his heart out. Quite an unusual sight!

Sue Moore NORTHFIELD, MINNESOTA

UP NORTH
The boreal owl, an elusive resident of the northern forest, rarely wanders south of Canada.

When we received an influx of irrupted owls from the North, I spent every spare moment exploring our more remote locales on snowshoe. By birding this way, I stumbled across this little boreal owl, only about 10 inches tall. It seemed equally curious about me and remained perched here for 90 minutes or so. Darkness came, and we went our separate ways. I'm glad I spent the time, because although I returned to this spot several times, I never saw a boreal again.

Ken Greshowak DULUTH, MINNESOTA

A few winters ago, we had about two dozen starlings at our feeders at once. This particular bird was adept at protecting one side of the feeder, keeping the others away. The stars on its feathers were so pretty against the snow.

Mary Baird
TRAFALGAR, INDIANA

We have several bird feeders outside our dining room windows, enabling my husband and me to watch birds throughout the day. The devotion this particular pair of cardinals show to each other is simply enchanting. After they ate some seeds together, they landed in a nearby pine tree, and I had to take a portrait of the lovebirds.

Melissa Boele
MANSFIELD, ARKANSAS

It was incredibly exciting to capture this cedar waxwing tossing a crabapple into the air at just the right moment. The bird's behavior was interesting to observe. The waxwing didn't eat every crabapple—it punctured each one with its pointy tongue to taste the fruit first. Then it discarded some and ate the others.

Gary Detonnancourt
HARRISVILLE, RHODE ISLAND

This was a new visitor to my backyard: a white-breasted nuthatch! The bird took an interest in the feeder I'd recently hung, and I had fun trying to capture a photo.

Ashley Maris
GRANTS PASS, OREGON

Northern cardinals are always a welcome sight. They decorate
the landscape with a pop of red as they sit atop the branches like fluffy ornaments.
They're so refreshing when it's dreary.

Deanna Mayhew CROCKER, MISSOURI

LOVE SONGS
Most woodpecker drumming in late winter is done to court potential mates; they are singing to declare their territory.

While taking pictures of a male downy woodpecker, this female decided to investigate my intrusion on her peaceful morning. She hopped from one log or branch to another until she settled on a dead tree trunk. It was as if she was posing for my camera. I love how she seems to be daring me to take her picture.

Dennis Peters DEARBORN HEIGHTS, MICHIGAN

On a cold winter's day in Ohio, I snapped this shot of a mourning dove with my Canon PowerShot SX60 HS. With its feathers fluffed and eyes closed, this adorable bird seemed to be finding some comfort and rest while perched on a crabapple tree in our backyard.

Sheila Hernandez
LIMA, OHIO

Across the street from my house is a church that has a number of bushes with berries. Every year, for about two days, a bunch of robins come to feed. I always keep an eye out for them. This is one of the shots I managed to get during last year's visit.

William Friggle
DENVER, PENNSYLVANIA

Waking up to find hoarfrost covering the trees was a wonderful surprise on a cold February morning. Despite the temperatures, this American tree sparrow had found a patch of sunshine and seemed to be enjoying itself.

Patty Jennings
STACYVILLE, MAINE

We were exploring the Wheeler National Wildlife Refuge in Alabama one January when this sweet golden-crowned kinglet popped up right next to us on the trail. At first, it was too close for me to even take its picture!

Kristy Baker
ROCKVALE, TENNESSEE

I waited all winter for this noble varied thrush to come close enough for a portrait. The bird skirted the edge of my property, just outside of camera range, searching for food. It wasn't until a rare snowfall covered its feeding grounds that it came to see what I was serving at my feeders.

Sally Harris CARLSBORG, WASHINGTON

FLOCKING TOGETHER
In the winter, house finches join mixed flocks with pine siskins and goldfinches.

A few weeks before Christmas, a heavy snow fell and birds flocked to my feeding station. I love bird-watching and photography, so I bundled up and went outside to wait for the perfect shot of these house finches.

Robyn Battenfield MUSKOGEE, OKLAHOMA

A black-capped chickadee posed on this festive basket that I made.

Respah Mitchell
EXETER, MAINE

This partial albino female cardinal began visiting my feeder. She is so beautiful, and I am so lucky!

Kathy Freeborn
WEST GROVE, PENNSYLVANIA

As I was easing along a waterway, I looked over and saw a green heron standing on one leg. The bird was extremely still and quiet. I carefully slipped through the brush and captured this photo before it flew off. It sure was a beauty!

Jim Amrine
MESA, ARIZONA

A male and female northern yellow-shafted flicker visited last winter, first arriving in the fall. I captured this photo of the male landing with his wings spread out. Just look at the gorgeous gold shafts in his feathers!

Sherry Akins
FREDERICK, MARYLAND

This sweet Anna's hummingbird found a home in our garden one winter. I wanted to take a picture, then had the idea of putting an ornament on the branch where our feathered friend liked to perch. When snow started falling, I waited patiently, and soon she came and sat in just the right place. What a marvelous way to say Merry Christmas!

Natalia Karapunarly SALEM, OREGON

Snowy owls have been on my photographic bucket list for years. When I heard that someone spotted one in my area, I made the trek to the beach. This owl was perched on a washed-up tree stump approximately 50 yards from me. The light broke through the clouds, and I was at last able to capture images of the regal creature.

Donald Mroczkowski ERIE, PENNSYLVANIA

I looked out the window

during a winter storm and saw an eastern bluebird sitting on my Fraser fir tree. I grabbed my camera and quietly slipped out on the deck to snap this photo. I returned a few minutes later to fill the feeder and the bluebird was still there. Perhaps this bird was one of the summer babies returning for a snack!

Mary Lou Jubin
NORTON, OHIO

I see dark-eyed juncos almost

daily in my backyard. Although I know they can be found on much of the continent, it seems as if they are all residing here in North Carolina! The juncos mostly feed on the ground, but occasionally they fly to the feeders or use my birdbath. I think they're adorable!

Kimberly Miskiewicz
RALEIGH,
NORTH CAROLINA

Welcome Winter Birds

Become host to a bevy of backyard visitors with these cold weather tips.

House finch

Attracting your favorite feathered friends in winter requires extra effort. But it will be worth it when songbirds arrive, making your snow-covered yard merry and bright.

Go nuts!

Many backyard favorites, such as chickadees, woodpeckers, nuthatches and brown creepers, love to snack on peanut pieces. Mix them with seed, or hang a special peanut feeder to attract extra attention. Peanuts in the shell are blue jay favorites. Watch for fussy jays to pick up several peanuts before choosing the perfect one.

PROVIDE SHELTER

When all the leaves have dropped and most trees and shrubs are bare, it's hard for birds to find a safe habitat for roosting and shelter. It's easy to create a winter comfort zone by growing evergreen trees, bushes, vines and ground covers. Don't forget to leave up a few birdhouses, too.